Refactored

My Attempt at Breaking into Tech During the Rise of the Coding Boot Camp

A memoir by Sean Rogers

Refactored: My Attempt at Breaking into Tech During the Rise of the Coding Boot Camp
by Sean Rogers

First Edition: May 2021

Published by Onyx Neon Press
www.onyxneon.com

Editor: Chastity West
Cover design: Phil Poole

This book was typeset on Ubuntu using Pandoc and LaTeX. Many thanks to the open source developers who make these and other projects possible.

Follow the author:
Facebook: RefactoredMemoir
Twitter: @Sean_T_Rogers

ISBN: 978-0-9854519-8-1

To Jenny and Afton, who are in the background of this book but in reality are the main characters. I love you both.

Notes About this Book

This is a work of nonfiction based on my experiences attending a coding boot camp. Dates, times, locations, and other facts are told from memory, supplemented by interviews with some who were at the boot camp with me. Most names and some characteristics and backgrounds of people have been changed. In some cases, the names of companies have been changed.

The content and opinions shared within this book are solely my own and do not reflect the views or opinions of my employer or of Tech Elevator.

There is some code in this book. If there are mistakes in this code, you'll have to forgive me. I'm new here…

| Chapter One |

I'VE always wanted to be smart. In their twenties, people spend a lot of time trying to appear cool or artsy or cultured. And I tried to be those things, too, I'm not denying it. But really, deep down, I just wanted people to think I was smart. I still do. In my greatest fantasies, someone walks away from a conversation with me and tells their friend, "That guy is really smart." The friend nods in agreement, looking back with a mixture of awe and jealousy at my cool, effortless acumen.

To be clear, that doesn't happen. And it never will.

But I do know a lot about books, and knowing a lot about books makes it easier to dupe people into thinking you're smart. Being up-to-speed on the literary scene, you acquire arrays of information in small tidbits. These pebbles of information, judiciously cobbled in conversation, can often be enough to build a facade of high intelligence. I've become skilled at this trick, mainly because I had so much time to practice it. I worked in a bookstore for sixteen years. Among other factors, my desire to appear smart kept me in the bookstore over the long haul. And later, that same desire drove me to take the biggest risk of my life—going into considerable debt and pushing myself and my family to the brink of stressful chaos in an attempt to roughhouse my way into the world of computer software.

But let's back up. I began working at Barnes & Noble in the winter of 2002 shortly after exiting a hellish copywriting position in Secaucus, New Jersey. I was out of college six months and had already quit my first job.

I wanted to write fiction. Knowing I couldn't make any money writing fiction, I took a job at the Flatwater, New Jersey Barnes & Noble making a quarter above minimum wage. I worked there less than a year and then transferred across the Hudson into New York, to Forest Hills, Queens, where I became a manager. I stayed in New York for about five years and then moved back to Pittsburgh, Pennsylvania where I had grown up. I was newly married, set on buying a house, starting a family, and writing the novel that would get my name on a bookshelf and prove, beyond question, that I am smart.

I was set. I didn't make much money during those sixteen years (at the lowest $7.25 an hour and $20.00 at the height), but I didn't really care. While my friends bemoaned their vampiric jobs, I alone stated that I would happily work at Barnes & Noble until retirement. I meant it.

Glenn, the store manager of my Barnes & Noble, paged me from the receiving room on Monday morning. I knew something was wrong by the tone of his voice. We weren't friends, exactly, but we got along well and respected each other. He was red-eyed and haggard as I entered the office. He closed the door behind me.

I tried to remember if there was any misdeed I had committed that would call for a closed-door discussion. Did I make a joke that offended someone, I wondered. Had I taken an advance copy that I actually should have paid for? Was there something—some mistake—that I could clarify for Glenn and make his dour expression soften?

"Barnes & Noble is laying people off."

I raised my eyebrows.

"Really?" I prodded, not certain if he was laying me off or asking me to help him lay off others. Both options were horrid.

"Restructuring. Your whole position is being taken away," he said quietly. His red eyes were wet now. He looked at the wall behind me. "I'm really sorry about this."

My face pin-prickled. There was a sense of surreality.

"And they don't want to move me to another position?" I asked. I didn't want to make this harder on Glenn than it had to be, but come on. I was an excellent employee. "I'm coming off of two 'Exceeds Standards' reviews."

"Yeah, no," he mumbled. "It's just laid off."

Glenn went on to explain about severance and extended health care and that he would be a reference for whatever job I moved onto. I ended the conversation as quickly as I could. I retrieved my coat, the book I was reading, and my lunch, uneaten, packed an hour before. Glenn stayed in the office while I gathered my things; I was saved the indignity of being escorted from the building. As I exited through the double doors I heard Glenn page Betsy, the next in line for his sad hatchet job.

I called my wife from the car.

"What's up?" Jenny asked.

"I just got laid off."

I've always been a pull-the-bandaid-off kind of guy.

"What?"

"I got laid off," I said again.

It sounded like a joke or a lie. I didn't quite believe it myself. I was thirty-eight years old and had been at the job since I was twenty-three.

"Really?"

"Yeah. I'm coming home."

When I got home, the embarrassment set in. This job, which I liked but wasn't necessarily proud of, didn't value me. They viewed me as excess, best to be disposed of. In short, I wasn't good enough for the bookstore.

I had to tell Afton, my seven-year-old daughter, when she got home from school. She tried to joke around about it, a trait of Jenny's that she did her best to mimic, but I wasn't in the mood. I reacted sullenly and she wandered off to play Barbies, resurfacing just before dinner to inquire whether we were now poor.

The severance that Glenn had mentioned was pretty good. I was given sixteen weeks of full pay, one for each year of service. There was time.

After some careful consideration about my next move, I decided to dedicate a week to completely flipping out. I didn't sleep, exercised excessively, and nervously clicked through the Internet for long stretches. It was nice.

I rewrote my résumé for hours on end, wondering how much lying I could get away with. I scoured the job boards online and wrote to friends on Facebook whom I hadn't contacted in years. I spent every second of the day thinking about how I was going to make money. I considered freelance writing, working as a test driver of automated cars, getting a job at another bookstore, substitute teaching, being a ranger at a national park, learning how to be a roofer, and becoming a ringside judge for boxing and mixed martial arts. You know, all the grounded, reasonable career paths that anyone would look into when choosing a new line of work.

Before I applied to this motley lineup of positions, a few friends called with offers at their places of work. They were shitty jobs, every last one of them, but their very existence had a calming effect. After some serious drinking, I came to understand that I would be able to get back into the workforce whenever I chose. I would only be unemployed for as long as I cared to be unemployed. With this realization came a query I hadn't previously considered: When am I ever going to get four months of full pay and no work? Answer: Never again. I then made a decision that set my mind at ease. I would not even think about getting a job for a couple months, work on my novel, and take it easy.

And that's what I did. I had about one hundred pages of a fantasy novel I had started some years before, and between February and May of 2018 I pushed that tally over five hundred. Pretty good work.

A friend of mine and ex-Barnes & Noble employee had been made the director of a new grocery store opening in Pittsburgh. Green Basil, it was called. He had written to me on Facebook offering a job a few times, and as my walkabout months drew to a close, I accepted.

I had had a theory, ever since quitting that hellish copywriting job in Secaucus all those years ago, that I didn't much care to have a big and important job, a job that would rake in the dough but stress me out. For me, a regular job wasn't my path to success. I needed all of my brain waves saved up so that I could write full force. And I kept this theory alive as I went into the grocery business. The plan was to show up every day, do my work, and then return home in the early afternoons with plenty of time and plenty of mental fortitude with which to write the great American novel. Sure, it wasn't the bookstore, but it was simple, honest work. How bad could it be?

Answer to that question? Really bad.

Look, Green Basil is a perfectly good grocery store and I'm not saying you shouldn't buy your food there. But I am, with deadly seriousness, advising you not to work there.

I was the receiving manager, the same position that I had held at Barnes & Noble for the last few years of my employment. I was given a cache of bright green shirts that I had to wear every day, even though I was not customer-facing. The shirts had the Green Basil emblem on the front, a yellow plaque stating the name of the store accompanied by a silhouetted farmer atop a tractor, and corny phrases such as "Let the good thymes roll" and "I yam what I yam" written across the back.

The job wasn't great for my self-image. I try not to tie my ego to my work, but this effort is not always successful. When I moved back to Pittsburgh in 2008, one of my biggest misgivings was telling people that I worked at Barnes & Noble or, God forbid, running into old acquaintances at the store while I was working. I'm aware that I'm sort of an asshole for feeling this way. Barnes & Noble was a perfectly fine job. I've already stated emphatically that I enjoyed being employed there. But some vain recess of my soul whispered that I was somehow above that station, despite all visible proof. *This isn't what a smart person does for a living*, the vain voice told me.

I climbed past this personality defect long before February 2018, when I was laid off. Sometime after the birth of my daughter, I found a well of self-respect that came from a more primal place. Having a child spawned the acceptance and realization that I was a grown man, and my misgivings about my place in the world fell away for the most part.

But still. Driving back from a weekend in Toronto with two of my friends, at the border, the officer wanted everyone in the car to say what they did for a living. "I teach history," Mike said. "I'm a director for the Red Cross," Tim replied. "I work at a grocery store," whispered Sean, red with bruised vanity.

I yam what I yam.

At Green Basil, I spent the days unloading trucks into the back room and squeezing thousand-pound palettes of Fuji apples, Rainier cherries, and Barlett pears into the produce cooler. I delved into the freezer a dozen times a shift, an arctic locker so cold that your nose hairs froze with each breath. I choked back vomit as I chucked outdated rotisserie chickens down the garbage shoot, knowing that I would live with the smell of putrefying flesh until the dumpster was changed out on Friday.

When I wasn't cramming food into every centimeter of the back room, I was furiously inputting manifests of the deliveries into the early '90s spreadsheets that Green Basil ran its business on. I stared into the white screen, flies landing on my face like I was one of those poor children from the Sally Struthers infomercials, focusing with all my might to work typo-free, knowing that I would have to start typing the long columns of product numbers all over if the totals didn't add up at the end.

I went home each day dirty, the smell of rotting fruit and cow blood in my nose, and mentally exhausted. The writing did not go well that spring.

It might not seem like it from what you've read so far, but I can be tiresome with my positivity. Not all the time, mind you, but some of the time. There are areas in my life where I have turned a blind eye to the negative aspects and smiled my way through, citing hard work and a good attitude as an eventual savior. And that's what I was doing in June 2018.

"It's fine," I said to Jenny after a ten-hour day spent typing manifests into spreadsheets.

"It's okay," I reported, following an afternoon of lifting damp turkeys, dripping with plasma, from their cardboard crates.

"I think I can keep doing this," I insisted, having discovered a slew of maggots in my sock after a shift of wrestling with the broken trash compactor.

One particularly trying day, I was in the back room when I heard someone beating against the wall. I stopped what I was doing and listened. It was almost tribal, the beat, something I had heard in the New York subway systems from the men with plastic buckets upturned. Then someone screamed.

It was beastial, this scream. As if a god had died.

I ran to the bathroom and dashed through the swinging door. The drumming had begun again. Someone was in the stall, the door locked. I waited in horror, watching myself in the mirror of the restroom, as the redoubtable beat echoed across linoleum.

"Excuse me. . . ?" I tested.

The drumming stopped.

"Are you all right?" I asked.

"Mmmmm. . . I'm fine."

The voice was deep and gargled, but I recognized it as belonging to Bobby, the new produce guy, part-time.

"Do you need help or anything?"

"Nope...fine."

Bobby was supposed to start work in fifteen minutes and had, it turned out, decided to use heroin in the bathroom beforehand. High out of his mind, he had been drumming on the toilet lid.

"I'm going to need to find another job," I told Jenny that evening.

But what to do?

I thought that working at Green Basil might be similar to the back room at Barnes & Noble—the trucks, the solitude, the lack of customers. But it wasn't. I was at Barnes & Noble for the books, not because I had a driving passion about shipping and receiving. All of my skills were in retail management and I did not want to do retail management if it didn't have to do with books. So what could I do?

I struggled with this question. All I really wanted to do was write, but in sixteen years of writing I had made approximately $6,000 through publications. That probably wouldn't cut it, budget-wise.

Once, in my late twenties, when I was thinking about leaving Barnes & Noble, I had the wild idea to go back to school and become a math teacher. I am not good at math. And I don't particularly like it. But, to me, there was something romantic about attacking my weak point, hammering at it until it became a strength. I actually looked into what type of schooling I would need to make this path doable. It was a long road for someone with an English degree and the idea faded away.

But that same romantic feeling hit me again in July 2018 while driving to my parents' house for dinner. Tech Elevator, a coding boot camp new to Pittsburgh, bought a sponsorship on NPR. I had heard the commercial before but hadn't given it much credence. But now, sitting at a red light, I cocked my head in bemused thought. What if I learned how to code?

I posed that same question to Jenny when I met up with her and my daughter at my parents' house.

"What if I learned how to code computers?" I asked.

It was an absurd suggestion.

She shrugged her shoulders. "Yeah. Do it."

| Chapter Two |

I don't even like computers. Not really. And I wouldn't describe myself as a "technical person." The old idea of the math-teacher challenge resurfaced in my mind. What if this technical weak point became my career?

I had some close friends who were computer programmers, Michael and Elizabeth, a couple. I asked them what they thought of the idea one day as we had drinks on my porch.

"You could definitely do it," Elizabeth assured me.

"It's not that hard?" I asked.

"Well. . ."

The two of them recommended some websites—Free Code Academy and W3Schools Online Tutorials.

"Try it out," Michael suggested. "See what you think."

So I did. I liked the W3Schools website better, so I went with that one. I looked at some HTML, the bones of a website. I looked at some CSS, the appearance of a website. I looked at some JavaScript, the lightning that brings the digital Frankenstein to life. "Hmm," I sniffed. "Sorta cool."

I almost failed the online test for Tech Elevator, nearly squashing the idea right then and there. The test consisted of twelve logic questions, confusing little twisters rooted in algebra, the type of which I've never spent much time noodling over. I scored a seven out of twelve, which I found out some months later is the lowest score one can have and still apply. Jenny took it for fun. Perfect score.

Tech Elevator regularly held open houses for prospective students, so I attended one in early August 2018. The school is located on the North Side of Pittsburgh in a somewhat hip urban area dotted with a few good bars and several interesting restaurants. On the top floor of The House of Metal, an old warehouse converted into offices, the Tech Elevator space is tucked back in the corner, about two thousand square feet of hardwood, black screens, and neatly coiled cords.

With a long hallway at the entrance, it opens up with a large classroom and two offices to the left. To the right, a spacious common room with couches, chairs, and a kitchenette housing an island at the far end. The open area is the Elevate Space, as the TE employees call it, and the word "ELEVATE" is spelled out in rusty letters resting on the ledge of a vast series of windows pointed to the southern cityscape. It's very clean, very modern, what you'd expect a cool startup in San Francisco to look like. This is by design, of course, as is the brewing coffee, the JavaScript scrawled on the window with dry-erase marker, the ping pong table, and the six-pack of locally brewed IPAs resting on the countertop in the kitchenette.

I quietly took a seat at one of the round tables. The show began with a video about Pittsburgh, shown in the light of a city on the verge of a tech explosion—thousands of tech jobs opening up every year and only hundreds of qualified candidates to fill them. The numbers that the school boasted were unbelievable—a 92 percent placement rate and average salaries above $58,000. And after each statement they addressed the elephant in the room: Can I *really* learn to code in just three and a half months? *Yes*, they insisted.

I went home, my head buzzing with inscrutable code and dollar signs. I know my stampeding positivity always runs the risk of slipping into gullibility, so I had Jenny turn her skeptical eye on the business. Was this place for real?

Coding boot camp scams can happen, at least to some degree. There is a non-profit group called the Council on Integrity in Results Reporting (CIRR) that has taken a special interest in online schooling and coding boot camps to make sure this doesn't happen. The CIRR reports on things like how many students graduate on time, how many are working outside the field they studied, and how many are working part-time jobs. They do their best to keep these programs honest.

The problem is these schools self-report. Some coding boot camps fudge the numbers. They might count jobs that are only within shouting distance of tech as a success. A part-time support job might be counted toward their above 90 percent placement rating. Some coding boot camps have been known to hire "teaching assistants" when they could not place certain students, and these teaching assistants buff their placement numbers. Others have even been known to not count a student as a graduate until they have successfully found a job.

And even when they're not a scam, the boot camps are a business. They want classes full of paying students. The good news is that, if everything is on the up-and-up, the incentives in place should work in favor of the student. The students want the good paying jobs and the boot camps want the impressive statistics.

After a thorough few days of Internet muckraking, Jenny came back with the opinion that, yes, it was legitimate. There was a bad review or two floating out there, but the overwhelming proof was that this place could get you a job. And a good one.

The main misgiving that Jenny had was that I would dislike the work. And that was a reasonable misgiving, as I had never shown an inkling of interest toward code or computers. If anything, I tended to shun newer tech and held on to CD players and flip phones long past the point of prudence. But what I do like, I argued, is to learn.

Part of why I like to read is because I like being good at trivia. I also sometimes listen to podcasts of classes at Harvard and Yale, getting some free education on philosophy or certain periods of history. Also, I'm a multi-instrumentalist—I usually learn a new instrument every two or three years. In fact, I had just begun kicking around the idea of learning to play the accordion. But why not learn JavaScript instead? It would certainly pay better. I applied. So long, polka.

Within twenty-four hours of applying I had an interview scheduled. I met Caitie Zajko, the Pathway director at Tech Elevator, for the first time. I immediately liked her. She reminded me of my sister, except with the intensity turned up to eleven. Caitie is slight of build, exact in the way she speaks, and direct. She has a conversational style that makes me feel hopeful, positive, and somehow nervous all at once. In short, she seems like someone who gets shit done.

I spoke with her for a good bit and then took a second logic test, this time on an actual piece of paper. I was nervous about this test because I had done so poorly on the first one, but I shouldn't have been. After my dubious online performance, I looked up the questions and figured out how to solve them. Many of the same questions, or ones of their ilk, reappeared in the live test. I never did get my score for that one, but it felt like I did really well.

I took the test on Wednesday and lived with no small amount of anxiety for the remainder of that week and all through the weekend. I wasn't sure what the competition was like to get into the school, and I wasn't sure if I could afford it even if I did get in. Jenny wanted me to research Academy Pittsburgh, another coding boot camp that was much cheaper, but my heart was set on Tech Elevator.

I was still working at Green Basil and the job had grown particularly unbearable. Through an ordering mishap, we ran out of room in our freezers. We rented three freezer trucks, which I was tasked with managing. For weeks, I moved trucks around the parking lot, large behemoths that I was not qualified to drive. I climbed in and out of the freezer trucks, digging through the stiff, icy cardboard to find certain cuts of meat. The amount of gas the trucks burned was wildly inconsistent depending on how often the freezer door had been open. I had to call a special company to come out and fill them each time they were low on fuel, and if I didn't call in time we lost thousands of dollars worth of food. It was a nightmare.

So when Caitie called me around noon the following Monday and offered me a spot, I felt as if a pressure valve had been released somewhere in my brain. The cohort started January 19. I had six months left at Green Basil. Just six months. I could do anything for six months and the clock was ticking. Just for fun, I set a countdown on my phone for January 19, right then and there, just after my call with Caitie. Tick tick tick...

Caitie offered me a place in the fall cohort, which started in just a few weeks. This was tempting, but I didn't think I'd be prepared for that one. There was studying to do, money to be mustered, and a job to quit. I probably could have gotten it together and attended the earlier session, but for many reasons it was a good thing I didn't. The fall of 2018 was like a roller coaster ride. Like a roller coaster ride if roller coasters were not fun at all and instead were engineered as an attempt to ruin your life.

It began with the damn roof. There had been water dripping all summer up in the attic but now, when it rained, it came into our bedroom and literally fell right in our faces as we slept. Something had to be done about this.

Money was tight, and it was only going to get tighter, but we had no choice. The roof had to be replaced. We took out a loan and hired a company to do the work. Not forty-eight hours after the work was finished, water leaked into our bedroom once more. When one of the workers came to check it out, he reported that it was the box gutters and not the roof that was leaking. "OK," I said, "so can you just fix that yourself or do you need the crew?"

No. The box gutters are not included in the roof. We could call someone else to fix the box gutters. It would cost somewhere in the range of $4,000.

I'm not someone who yells. But I spent the next month on the phone being passed around from one person to another associated with the roofing company demanding that they stop the leak. Each person would pass me on to the next, telling me that it would be fixed soon. This went on for weeks. Each time it rained water fell into my bedroom and into my daughter's bedroom. At work, looking out the back door as it poured in the early afternoon, I boiled with fury.

They eventually capitulated, but it dragged on from August to late September. Every day, me complaining to someone on the phone after a long day of shitty work. Every time it rained, our bedroom ceilings taking on the look of a dunked graham cracker.

Also during this time, Jenny's father was growing more and more ill. He had suffered a litany of issues over the course of his peculiar life—prostate cancer, a serious motorcycle accident, triple by-pass heart surgery, diabetes. He was also once shot in the neck in a street fight, a story I have heard told many different ways over the years, all of which are suspect. But over the course of the past two years, it had become clear that a degenerative lung disease was what would finally do in this tall-tale-of-a-man.

As Russ struggled with shortness of breath and a low oxygen count, as he went from being active to not being able to walk a few city blocks, as he eventually succumbed to the wheelchair he'd been rejecting for half a decade, our visits to Ohio increased.

By early September, some amalgamation of our family was visiting every weekend. All three of us would go on Friday night. Or just Jenny and Afton would visit, from a Thursday till Sunday. Jenny would make the three-hour drive by herself on a Saturday morning, the car silent except for the drumming of her fingers on the steering wheel, wondering if he would still be alive by the time she got there.

Russ entered the hospital in October knowing he wouldn't see the outside again. But he kept making plans. He wanted to go to Vegas one last time. He wasn't allowed to fly, so they would drive, or maybe take a train through the mountains. Hooked up to an IV, a tube pulling and shushing over his mouth to keep him oxygenated, he wasn't fooling anyone.

Russ died in the middle of October, days after my daughter's birthday, and we mourned him in Fremont, Ohio, among crowds of relatives and friends. Less than a week after returning from the funeral, I entered the hospital myself.

I like to think I'm a healthy person. I eat fruit and vegetables with my meals and I exercise almost every day. I used to smoke cigarettes, but quit some months before Afton's birth, nearly nine years prior. I probably drink too much, but I have no desire to solve that problem and believe wholeheartedly that my combined good habits trump this one not-so-good one.

The thing is, I have diverticulitis. What is diverticulitis? I don't really know, honestly. And neither, in my opinion, do doctors. What happens is that little pockets in my intestines become continually infected and inflamed. When it's mild, it feels like my belt is always too tight. When it's bad I crouch fetally and binge on painkillers.

I learned to control it pretty well after having a flareup in January, just before getting laid off from Barnes & Noble. Any time I felt it coming on, I went on a liquid diet for a handful of days. One good thing about working at Green Basil (maybe the only good thing?) is that they have an amazing salad bar. I ate from it almost every day. Midway through July, I felt so good that I thought I would never have problems with diverticulitis again.

But in the days following Russ's death, when we were hanging around Jenny's mom's house for a week with nothing to do but eat all of the food the neighbors kept bringing us, I had a relapse. I was fine while still in Fremont, but the Monday morning when I went back to work I felt it returning, like a childhood bully just back from summer camp. Tuesday of that week was terrible. I kept the top button of my jeans undone to relieve some pressure and stayed seated at the computer as much as I could. I had only been at the Green Basil job for four months and I had just taken off ten days in a row. I couldn't call out sick now, just when I'd returned. I stopped eating and planned to tough it out.

On Wednesday morning I was unable to bend over to tie my shoes because I was in so much pain. This should have been an indicator that toughing it out was not an option. I should have called in sick. Instead, I tucked my shoelaces into the sides of my shoes and drove to work, the seat leaned back like a '90s rap video so that I didn't have to fold my abdomen.

I gave up halfway through the day. I told my boss what was going on and drove home. Taking a fistful of Advil, I climbed into bed, intending to fast and sleep my way through it. I woke up about two hours later and had the type of fever where reality becomes liquid. It was time to seek medical help.

I drove to a Med Express. I laid down, shirt off, the feverish skin of my back against the crinkly paper as the doctor kneaded the muscles of my stomach.

"You have to go to the emergency room," she reported almost immediately. "You have inflamed intestines. If something bursts, you could go septic."

"Septic?"

"Yes."

"What does that mean?"

"It means you will be poisoned by your own waste."

And so I leaned back into my car and made my way to the emergency room with a belly full of fire.

Naked but for my hospital gown and waiting for a nurse to enter the room, I dreaded the moment when Jenny would arrive. She had had enough of hospitals and sickness over the last six months. Just when it had finally, painfully, come to an end, I was dragging her back in. She had been in the room when her dad died. Hurt and damage were accrued as she witnessed the man who raised her struggle in panicked confusion during the last minutes of his life. Jenny wasn't over the pain, not by a long shot. It might take decades for her to heal, if she ever did. But especially now, just back to life after a month of death, everything was too fresh.

I couldn't talk when she came in. Tears streamed from my eyes and my throat grew sore. This emotion probably scared her more than was necessary—an indication that I had some incurable disease rather than digestion problems. But I couldn't stop. I had hardly slept for two days, hadn't eaten either, and had been in no small amount of pain the entire time. I broke down.

But morphine helped out. That stuff's crazy! My neck muscles stopped working the moment it hit my veins. My head fell back and my eyes rolled like the junkies in Trainspotting. The pain in my stomach drifted away and things became gummed up and weird.

I can't say why I was surprised when the doctor insisted I be admitted to the hospital. You don't usually get morphine if they're planning on sending you home in an hour. But I was shocked. I expected them to check me out, prescribe some antibiotics, and send me on my way. No, sir. Get comfortable. This was the first night I would ever spend in a hospital.

I went in on Wednesday and didn't get out till Sunday. I had antibiotics through an IV and a steady stream of morphine. I fasted until Saturday morning, and then ate only toast and tomato soup. But I felt a lot better. There had been talk of surgery, but my quick recovery squashed the idea. It was nice to get home.

I was back in the hospital within a week. Back on a liquid diet. Back on morphine. And, the worst part was, I wasn't going to escape the knife this time. I was destined for surgery.

Having a needle in your arm for a week is a unique experience. Anyone can walk in the room, change what's in your IV bag, and it goes straight into your body, fucking you up with different chemicals. Just before the surgery, my IV was changed to anesthesia and paralytic. I left this world for some time.

Have you heard the horror story about the person who didn't get enough anesthesia and woke up during surgery? And they were paralyzed and so couldn't tell the surgeons that they were awake and they felt all the pain, every scalpel through every nerve? Well, that didn't happen to me. But I *thought* it did.

I woke up with bright lights above me and a tube down my throat. I tried to talk and gagged. Someone extracted the tube and I questioned frantically, "Did I wake up too soon? Is it over? Am I still in surgery?"

It was over. I was in a recuperating area where they watched my vitals and waited until it was safe for me to go back to my hospital room. This was a Tuesday. By Saturday I was sent home. I had spent my thirty-ninth birthday laid out in the hospital.

The recovery took about a month, but I had to go back to work within a few weeks. Green Basil was pretty good to me concerning the time off, but I had burned through any PTO they were willing to throw my way. Between October and November I missed over four weeks of work. And the worst part of getting out of the hospital? That's when the bills start coming.

We weren't broke. Not entirely, but close. I was making $4,000 less a year at Green Basil than I had been at Barnes & Noble, Jenny had switched jobs and lost a bit of salary in the jump, the bills for the roof loan had started coming in, and now there were bills from the hospital that could range anywhere from $100 to $1,000—and it was unclear what we owed and how many of these bills were coming. All of this made quitting my job and spending $15,000 on magic beans seem like a pretty stupid idea.

I hadn't quit my job yet or told anyone at Green Basil that I would be leaving. I had decided to give them a month's notice, so the second week of December loomed large in the near future. Should I stay at the job and try to save money so that I could, perhaps, join the summer cohort of Tech Elevator rather than the spring? Would I even be able to save money with our financial situation? I slouched to work every day wondering what to do, the massive cut that hadn't yet healed on my abdomen weeping through its bandage, giving me a daily red dot on all of my green work shirts. Let the good thyme's roll.

It was late December when the only good thing to happen all year happened. Russ had left some money for his children. Not oh-my-God-we're-rich money, but a good chunk. Combined with a loan my parents floated us, we would make it through the spring. So long as I *immediately* got a job upon graduating, we would be OK. No pressure or anything.

| Chapter Three |

THE night before January 19, 2019, I didn't sleep well. A head thick with anxiety, I worried whether I was smart enough to do this. The consequence of wanting to appear smart is that proof of the opposite becomes a constant fear. The crucible of a coding boot camp would reveal my inadequacies, and these inadequacies would be exposed to my little corner of the world.

I also worried whether it was the right choice to spend the money. With Russ's check, we could clear most of our debts and start fresh if I didn't go to school. And I worried, for some reason, about finding parking. I probably worried about the parking more than anything else in the wee hours of morning. There was no dedicated lot and this was the goddamned North Side. I pictured myself looping around and around the building looking for a spot while everyone else was inside becoming computer geniuses. My brain was fuzzy and my body was tossy-turny.

The parking, at least, was a non-issue. There were plenty of spots. As I walked around the city corner toward the House of Metal at eight in the morning, I eyed the other people moving my way. Was this the first glimpse of my fellow students, or were these just people on their way to work?

I took the elevator with a man named Jimmy. He had been at the open house I attended and, though I didn't speak with him, I remembered him from that evening. Everyone who attended that open house remembered Jimmy. He was tall and thin, with a skinny man's muscular frame and long, thick hair. He had a thin mustache, a wispy goatee and was prone to wearing board shorts and colorful tees. At the open house night, he came off as a hippy-surfer-type. He asked a question that at once revealed his entire personality. It was long and rambling, humble and funny. The drift of it was that he wasn't sure he would be smart enough to take the class and, even if he was, he wasn't sure he wanted a job in tech. Familiar territory, honestly. And, honestly, I imagine everyone else who attended the open house thought he probably *shouldn't* take the class. But here he was.

I nodded to him and he came back with a "What's up, friend?"

We rode the elevator together but didn't talk much more. He was cool and friendly, but he was nervous just like me. Jimmy's big personality was doing its best to tread lightly.

The glass door to Tech Elevator was wedged open, so Jimmy and I walked in. We were early. There were only seven or eight people there, the majority of them TE employees. There were bagels from Panera and coffee brewed from Commonplace, a local Pittsburgh coffee maker. I grabbed half a bagel and a coffee and sat down at a high top with an amber-haired man named Moshe. He wore a long beard down to the center of his chest and a yarmulke. He had thick glasses and bright blue eyes that seemed inquisitive, but when I said hello, he just murmured hello back and looked away, eventually becoming interested in his phone.

The room quickly filled with students. I studied them and they studied me, but we were a quiet bunch. I assumed everyone was terrified.

The director of Tech Elevator Pittsburgh, Kyle Warner, is a big man. He's tall with a neat, blond beard and thick glasses. He took the center of the room and introduced himself. He lauded us for our decision to attend the class, calling each of us brave, and then focused the attention around the group as we each said our name and one interesting thing about ourselves.

There had been some living done. Among the students there was a chef, a rock climber, a bassoonist, a yoga instructor, people who had lived in India, Japan, France, Russia, Scotland. Yes, there had been some living done and it was done in a relatively short amount of time. I was not the oldest one there, but a quick glance around told me that I was close to it. There were a few people I eyed up as being within a few years of me, but there were only two students, a woman in her mid-to-late forties and an older man with a head of white hair, who I was sure I was younger than. I had assumed this would be the case, but it was still flustering, as if I had walked into a concert and didn't understand the music these kids were listening to.

After we introduced ourselves, Kyle gave his second speech. This one focused more on what would happen over the duration of the cohort. Some of it was housekeeping, some of it introduction to staff, and some of it ground rules about how to treat each other and general social expectations. But the main focus was this: You will be challenged over the next fourteen weeks and you will be changed.

You will be changed.

It was somehow both inspiring and threatening at the same time.

We split up into our two separate classes. Tech Elevator offers courses on one of two programming languages, Java and .NET (read “dot net”). There are as many programming languages as there are pixels on a computer screen, but for the last decade or so these two languages have dominated. I chose .NET for no reason other than that was the language that my friend Elizabeth used at her place of work and I figured maybe she could give me a recommendation some time in the future.

It was interesting to see how the students split. Java was definitely the cool kids language. Aside from Rob, who was the aforementioned yoga instructor, all the man-buns and skinny jeans headed off to the Java room and all the stonewash and crewcuts stayed in .NET. At the outset, it appeared as if we were the dorkier classroom.

The .NET classroom was broken out into three long, white tables. Above each workspace was suspended a sleeping, black monitor, waiting for a student’s hand to nudge the mouse and wake it up. On the back of each black swivel chair was a Tech Elevator branded backpack, left there for us. It was pretty slick, I thought: black and sturdy with room for a laptop and notebooks, the name of the school written on it next to a blue circle with a white arrow inside pointing upwards. I needed a new bag. My old one was nearing its second decade.

On the desk in front of the swivel chairs were silver laptops, sleek and metal like a 1950s SciFi rocket. Rob’s tools—his computer and bag—were in the seat next to mine. He introduced himself and shook my hand. Short and fit, Rob is good-looking, with long hair tied in a bun and deep-set brown eyes. Within a week the other students would be referring to him as Jon Snow, because he looked so much like the actor from Game of Thrones. He spoke in a manner that seemed as if he were overcoming a great shyness. We made small conversation while we waited for things to begin, and when I spoke he listened intently, as if he were memorizing the words coming from my mouth.

Then, the Bill Reeves show began. Bill was the .NET teacher and had extensive experience working as a developer for Microsoft, traveling the world as an evangelist for new Microsoft products, and building several of his own apps, mostly about golf courses.

Bill is tall (most of the men working for TE are extremely tall for some reason) and stout, in his late fifties. He wears thick-rimmed black glasses. He is bald in the front and keeps a long, gray ponytail down the center of his back, which he claims he grew by accident while coding for months on end in his younger days. He is clean shaven and has the kind of mouth and speech patterns that are reminiscent of Jay Leno—that is to say, he is fast-talking, charming and clever, with the tenacity to tell the same jokes over and over, all with the distant hint of a mostly cured lisp.

Before Bill had us open our laptops, there was yet another introductory speech. Unlike the talk from Kyle, this one was easy-breezy, peppered with witticisms, the serious points reiterated as if they were one-liners.

"Don't make me be dad," Bill told us. "Get your work in on time."

He clicked through a presentation he'd put together, letting us know that we would have two days for each assignment. We could come to him with questions but he preferred we worked with each other first before asking him. Homework would be given a zero if not turned in, a one if turned in partially finished or with many incorrect answers, a two for satisfactory work, and a three for exceptional. If, halfway through the program, we were averaging less than a one, we could be asked to leave. Bill mentioned this casually as sixteen sets of eyes widened in fear. He clicked to the next slide.

The phrase "Say no to drugs!" was written on the next slide with a picture of McGruff, the Crime Dog. This is the only point where Bill got serious. "Guys, it's only fourteen weeks. Please, please, *please* do not lose a job over grass."

He was reiterating something Kyle had said earlier in the afternoon. When Kyle told the story, he revealed that a student from the last cohort had lost a job to a failed drug test. Kyle explained that most companies that drug test will test urine and that with our fourteen weeks of class we had plenty of time to stop smoking marijuana and pee clean. He added that the student who lost the job had lost it over a hair test, which the United States government sometimes gives to its prospective employees and can detect drug use within the past *six months*.

Now, the typical student at a coding boot camp is someone who is a different sort of thinker. They are usually on their second career, and their first career was typically something like waiting tables, working in retail, gigging as a musician, or some type of manual labor. They are also usually someone who takes a lot of risks and isn't afraid of new, uncomfortable things. Basically, it's the same description as your casual pot-smoker.

I'm not really into pot, but it happens. I was coming off a surgery just two months prior and had been on my best behavior while I healed, so I could have passed the urine test on day one. But six months? Not so confident.

And more than half the class felt like I felt. Rob turned pale as a winter north of the wall at the continued mention of drug tests. I imagined that the cool-kid Java class had even more to worry about.

Finally we were told to open our computers. The background was a pleasing blue with the TE symbol from my bookbag prominently displayed. I entered the user name and password that were written on a post-it stuck to my laptop and I was in.

Bill instructed us to open up a program called Git Bash.

"One of the most important tools that a programmer uses is their version control tool," he told us. "How do you manage five, ten, a *hundred* programmers all working on the same project? What if you have two people working on the same part of an app at the same time? What if you don't like the changes someone made and you want to go back to the way it was last week? That's what version control is for. And that's what Git Bash is: version control software."

There was a small window on my screen, a black, simple background with bright yellow, blue, and pink writing. The yellow writing looked to be a long file name and I couldn't identify the pink writing at all. It was nothing more than a jumble of letters and symbols, but it was a jumble that was pleasing to look at. I smiled to myself and glanced over at Rob. *We're doing it*, I thought, *we're coding*.

"Now type the word 'git'—g-i-t— and then the word 'pull,'" Bill told us.

Sixteen pairs of hands typed exactly what Bill told us to type.

"Now press enter."

I pressed enter and the git bash window went spastic. A percentage number started rapidly counting up from zero to one hundred, a line of red dashes then a line of green. White text scrolled like a bag of marbles dropped down the stairs.

Rob leaned over and looked at my screen and then back at his own.

"Are we going to understand all of this some day?" he asked.

I watched the multi-colored gobbledygook tumble down the screen. It seemed completely impossible that I would one day be able to watch this scroll of symbols and divine any kind of sense.

"I don't know," I whispered. "I really don't know."

Git is version control software, but it's also what's called a command line tool. It's a way to swiftly navigate and use the folder system of your computer. When you're clicking through the files in your computer with the pictures of manilla folders and the names you've given the files above them? That's called a GUI (pronounced "gooey") or a Graphical User Interface. In other words, there are pictures representing your files. The command line is text-based, not picture based, and is the preferred method for dealing with files in the programming world. The actual moving in and out of files is probably easier on the GUI. But while working with code, we're storing a master copy of a project in a repository separate from our computer. We can pull work from that master project, make changes, and then send our changes back to the master copy in the repository. Git makes this function much easier.

We were assigned homework of twenty questions, all to do with version control using Git. Honestly, it wasn't that hard. There are some complicated things one can do with Git such as branching multiple times from the master branch, stashing code to save later, and falling back to old versions. But none of that was included in the homework. It was mainly moving in and out of different files, making changes, and pushing those changes back to the master branch.

My biggest moment of fear was when I was told to type a tilde. A tilde is the symbol on the keyboard that looks like this: ~. I just couldn't find it. I held my hands in the air like a T. rex and stared at my computer for five solid minutes. It was such a stupid thing to ask that I couldn't bring myself to seek help. Right around the time it felt like I was going to have a full-blown panic attack over this little, squiggly line, I saw it hiding up to the left, just under the escape key. Everything was cake after that. I finished in about an hour, as did most of the class.

| Chapter Four |

STARING into his computer screen while sitting at the head of the room, Bill said "OK, quiz time!"

I had been reading over the homework about Git from the day before and looked up toward the teacher. Quiz? I didn't know there was going to be a quiz.

Bill walked us through signing on to a website called Socrative. We would sign onto Socrative every morning of the cohort and, more often than not, there were connection problems. (Socrative was gleefully nicknamed "Suckrative" by a former class. They had gone so far as getting the suckrative.com domain name and rerouting it to Socrative. As of this writing, it still works. Go ahead. Try it.). When Socrative was working, we first took a survey. The survey consisted of questions such as "How well did you learn yesterday's lesson?", "How well did you comprehend the reading?", and "What is your energy level for today?"

A quiz on yesterday's lecture followed the survey.

I felt my heartbeat in my temple as I took that first quiz. There were ten questions and I felt fairly confident about eight of them. There is immediate feedback on a Socrative quiz, not when you're finished but after each and every question. This can be good or bad depending on how you control your mental state. If you get frustrated with missing a question and let it affect your thinking, it isn't hard to drop the next one because you lost your temper. This would happen to me more than once.

But not this time. Ten out of ten.

I beamed to myself, way more proud than I had any right to be.

Once everyone was finished, Bill revealed a dashboard with the class's scores and I noticed that I was one of only two who scored perfectly. My head-size increased further. It was fortuitous that I had reviewed the previous day's homework just before the quiz. This definitely took me from an eight to a ten. I made a mental note to pull that trick each morning.

The day kept getting better. I was half-insane with coffee as I listened to Bill's lecture about variables, strings, ints, and doubles. My smile kept getting bigger and bigger as he talked, like an air mattress finding its shape as the pump hums. I started feeling comfortable. It was all familiar!

While watching the clock during my last six months at Green Basil, I studied the base levels of coding—HTML, CSS, and JavaScript. Once I decided that I was going to study .NET, I tried to find a way to learn about it.

Some facts about .NET: It's not actually a programming language. It's a framework built by Microsoft. A framework in programming is a collection of shortcut functionality built on top of (meaning "built with") some programming language. In a framework, there is a vast library of pre-programmed maneuvers that allow one to code faster and with fewer mistakes. .NET is usually paired with the programming language C# (read "see sharp"). So I hadn't signed up to learn .NET; I had signed up to learn C# using the .NET framework, .NET being a series of shortcuts that makes coding easier when applied to the C# language.

I didn't understand any of this before the second day of class when Bill explained it. This lack of knowledge made it pretty difficult to study leading up to the classes. Googling only works when you have a ballpark idea of what you're looking for. And even when I did manage to sleuth out that I might need to look into the language C#, I couldn't find a reliable way to access it. I was working on a Chromebook (I'm writing this, right now, on a Chromebook—please don't tell anyone), and every time I tried to take an online lesson there were files to download that my computer couldn't handle.

Not being able to study the actual language beforehand made me nervous. I'm someone who likes to be prepared. I lay out exercise clothes the night before. I carry a bottle opener wherever I go. I take dental floss when I hike. When I was a child, I used to play Final Fantasy on Nintendo with my best friend Nick, the kid next door. Before we went in to fight one of the big bosses, I would insist we wander around fighting random creatures for hours and hours so that we could gain experience points and become more powerful. Nick grew bored and wanted to continue with the game at a normal pace, but I insisted we keep engaging in repetitive fights and stack those experience points. When we finally had to face Lich, the Earth Fiend, we crushed him hard. The ease of the victory was deeply satisfying. So, yeah, the fact that I couldn't obsessively prepare for a .NET class kept me up some nights at the end of 2018.

But here I was, day two, and everything that came out of Bill's mouth made my head nod in knowing agreement, like a churchgoer on Easter. Booleans, decimals, setting variables and changing them—this is the stuff I studied for six months! I was hoping we'd explore HTML, which I'd really taken to, but sadly, that would be closer to the end of the course.

Homework was assigned after the lecture, but we didn't have a chance to look at it. After lunch, it was time for our first Pathway meeting. Pathway is the program at Tech Elevator that is concerned with job placement. It was the main reason I was attending Tech Elevator and not another coding boot camp or some online deal. This was the feather in TE's cap, the protector of their greatest boast—that they have a 92 percent placement rate and an average salary of $58,000.

The director of the Pathway Program was Caitie Zajko, whom I had met during the interview process. She had the feel of a big sister as she spoke (even though she's probably a decade younger than me). Caitie revealed the map the Pathway program would follow over the next fourteen weeks—setting up appropriate LinkedIn pages, conducting mock interviews, attending networking events, multiple rewrites of résumés, and crafting an elevator pitch, which was a short description of our journey that brought us to Tech Elevator and, hopefully, under the employ of someone's company.

Our time with Caitie and the Pathway program was way more stressful than the coding lectures. If something sounded difficult in the coding lecture, you peppered Bill with questions and he sussed it out with you until it made some type of sense. The technical stuff was confusing, but hard work would clarify all. On the other hand, there was nothing confusing about what Caitie was telling us to do. After that first talk with her, we all knew the deal. She wanted us to be friendly and professional, not just in person, but online as well. She wanted us to practice interviewing and public speaking. She wanted us to sell ourselves to employers. And to sell ourselves to employers, we had to know what we were selling.

She wanted us to figure out exactly who we were, to sit down, peer deep into the wells of our souls, and craft a story describing what we saw there.

In other words, what she was asking for was fucking impossible.

Her introductory speech made me super nervous. And I'm definitely on the more social end of the spectrum (that's a loaded word, but appropriate) when compared with the rest of the class. Moshe could barely make eye contact with anyone, what was he going to do? And I had identified at least five people in .NET alone who didn't seem to have any control over the volume of their voices.

Like everything else about the boot camp, the work with Pathway was going to happen quickly. We would start toiling on our elevator pitches next Monday and the first version of our résumé was due the following weekend. Just as we were breaking out the brown paper bags to hyperventilate into, Caitie introduced a team-building game. Time for fun.

We were split up into groups and mine was composed of three other people. We sat in a circle. To my right was Diane, a woman in her mid-to-late forties, personable and super fit. (She continued working as a personal trainer during the whole cohort.) To my left was a young man named Tim, also in really good physical shape (these computer geeks are more into exercise than the movies of the 1980s led us to believe) with short-cropped hair and a constant gloomy expression. Tim was an Ohio State University grad and a military veteran. He was good looking in a cold, mopy way—picture black and white ads in magazines with frowning male models and you'll be pretty close to picturing Tim. And across from me was Bradley, a dark-haired young man with a hobbit-like build and a constant, knowing smile, as if he had a secret about you and was waiting for the appropriate moment to reveal it. During his introduction the previous day, Bradley had announced to the class at large that he was from "bum-fuck Pennsylvania." I found this rather forward, as introductions go.

The team-building problem was this: We were stuck in the northern Canadian wildlands—a plane crash with four people and a strange list of items that might help us survive. The list included things like rope, a broken lighter, a Hershey bar, a suitcase full of clothes, a water bottle, a compass, a handgun. We were each told to privately prioritize which things would be most important for survival. I did my best to put together a reasonable list, putting the things that could keep us warm, fed, and hydrated toward the top. We also had a map, so I thought the compass was priority number one so that we could be certain of walking in the right direction toward the closest town.

We began the conversation and, of course, our priorities conflicted. Bradley thought the clothes were most important so that we could remain warm. Diane thought that anything with liquid in it—the water bottle, a bag of apples—would be the most essential items because of the threat of dehydration. All fair points.

"Do we need this gun?" Diane posed. "I ranked it at number eight, but I don't know. Do you guys think it's necessary?"

"I put it pretty low," Bradley said. "But, I guess we could run into bears or something?"

"I don't think we need the gun at all," I said. "People don't get attacked by bears too often, unless they're antagonizing them."

"And it's not like we're going to hunt or anything," Diane added.

"No," said Bradley.

I had put the handgun at number fourteen, ranked only above cornstarch.

I turned to Tim. He had been completely silent during the proceedings. "What do you think?"

"I put the gun at number one," he quietly reported.

"Oh."

There were about ten seconds of silence.

"So...why do you think the gun is the most important?" Bradley asked.

"I don't know," Tim said quietly. "I would just take it. If I was *really* there."

There was a certain horror-movie vibe to the way Tim said this.

As it turned out, we all would have died anyway. Each of us thought it was a solid idea to take the compass and start walking in the direction of the nearest town. This was wrongheaded. The compass was a trick. The real answer had it listed dead last. We should have made a camp and tried to signal the rescue plane that would surely be looking for us near the crash site. So.

After horribly dying in the wilderness, it was time to get back to coding. We had twenty problems that Bill had assigned earlier that morning. We pulled the file down from the repository using Git and got to work.

It wasn't hard. *Again*, it wasn't hard. A slow shock bloomed within my nervous system. Was I...good at this?

The questions involved simple things that I had already done during the second half of 2018. Set a variable and then change it. Make a mathematical expression and print the answer. Change a boolean to a string. There was one problem at the end that gave me a lot of trouble. In the problem Jim and Jan were attempting to paint many rooms in a large house. We were to use our newfound power of variables to figure out how many gallons of paint they would need to accomplish their feat. It was tough. I think I just didn't have the mathematical prowess to take a real shot at something like that. It went beyond the bounds of logic and into that technical realm of advanced numbers where I do not feel qualified to tread.

At least that's what I told myself. Most students finished the variable work in an hour or so and then spent the next two thinking over Jim and Jan. We worked together, we worked separately, some of us even asked Bill for help. No one figured out the correct answer.

But it was just one question. It's a strategy, we figured, on Tech Elevator's part, to give a little hint about how complicated things could become. But that stuff—the logic-so-complicated-it-makes-your-head-numb stuff—was way down the line.

That's what we told each other. We were very wrong.

| Chapter Five |

I get up early. Like, really early. Before five a.m. early. I began doing this shortly after my daughter was born.

Looking back, I can say that I had something of an epiphany in July 2011 when Afton was ten months old. She was a good baby, but we ran the sleep deprivation gamut, just like any parent does. She would fall asleep at 6:00 p.m. only to wake up hungry at midnight, she'd go down at 10:00 p.m. but wake up at four o'clock in the morning full of energy. We all know the game. But things turned around in the spring of 2011. She started sleeping through the night. We put her down at seven or seven thirty and we wouldn't hear her cooing complaints again until 6:00 a.m. It was blissful.

It ended at ten months. Afton straight-up stopped sleeping for more than two hours at a time. I used to sing her long songs while I tried to woo her unconscious, and I spent the months of May and June pacing the cracked hardwood floor of her nursery during the witching hours crooning "Tangled Up in Blue" and "Hallelujah" while Afton stared at me curiously, prepared with a well-rehearsed chorus of screams if I set her down.

There were two things that sent me over the edge that summer. The first was the failure of a novel I was trying to sell. It was called *God Bless the Mallards* and it was a sprawling history of a wealthy family who found themselves in the middle of every American wrong that had occurred over three hundred years—from the massacre of the American Indians to the conflict in Vietnam, coming to conclusion in the years after 9/11.

This might sound like an interesting premise, but believe me, you would not want to read it. The novel was a goddamn mess and no agent wanted to represent it.

This wasn't my first rodeo, far from it. I self-published a novel called *Ghost* at the tender age of twenty-four and then spent the next fifteen years trying to figure out the complicated Rube Goldberg machine of this finicky business that takes a one-hundred-thousand-word file from a person's computer and turns it into a bound tome upon a bookstore display. I kept getting hung up on one thing or another. Either I didn't understand how to write a good query letter or I wasn't able to summarize my work in two pages, or the story just plain wasn't good enough. I wrote eight novels between the ages of twenty-five and thirty-five and the attempted sale of each one was a slow, anxious death. I had a literary agent for a few years, but that didn't go anywhere.

This *God Bless the Mallards* failure, this one hurt. Maybe it was because I had spent so much time on it. My first draft clocked in at more than one hundred thirty thousand words (that's north of five hundred pages in a printed book), and I had worked tirelessly to whittle it down to a manageable hundred thousand. Maybe it was because I had finally figured out how to write an enticing query letter and had hooked several agents into requesting material, shooting my hopes into the stratosphere. Or, maybe it was because I hadn't slept.

Whatever it was, this one hurt.

The other problem was Jenny. She was worn down too. We moved from New York City to Pittsburgh at the end of 2008 and she had been working from home the whole time. Working from home is a luxury, sure, but it also means you make no office friends. She was in a new town and knew no one except my parents and a few of my old high school comrades I had cobbled together out of the distant past. During the summer of 2011, she tended to Afton during the day, trying desperately to work at her computer during the brief periods when there wasn't some essential piece of care she had to provide to our infant. By the time I got home from Barnes & Noble, she would have a dichotomous thirst for both companionship to counter the loneliness of the day and isolation so that she could finish her work.

I saw that she was hurting, depressed maybe, and suggested she take a trip with a friend—go away for the weekend while I take care of Afton.

The problem was, she didn't have any friends who weren't seven hours away. There was no one she could ring up and do something with to take advantage of my charitable whim. My suggestion highlighted this problem and fed into her hopelessness. She wrangled her mother from Ohio and they took a strange trip to southern Pennsylvania together. She came back more listless than when she left.

Jenny's inability to completely solve all of her problems with a single weekend away seemed pretty lazy to me. *If we had a weekend away*, I whispered to myself like Golem in his cave, *We would come back refreshed and happy, we would.* In my soured heart, I felt that my hard time was worse than her hard time, even though she was the one doing the majority of the work and spending hours and hours by herself. Had I lost touch with reality while wallowing in unearned self-pity? I mean, I don't know, maybe.

I let this, in combination with the book failure, send me tumbling. I felt really bad for myself. Again and again, I worked as hard as I possibly could, and again and again it bore no fruit. Feckless, unrealistic, and stupid, I watched the things that made me happy slipping away. I remember speaking with my friend Adeep on the phone, describing how I felt hollow all the time. If I had a feeling at all it was anxiety. My face was numb in the mornings, like a foot fallen asleep.

Then I turned it around. I turned it around by getting up early.

I've always been greedy about my time. On my perfect day, I have two hours to write and an hour to exercise. This greed was a real curse in my 2011 situation, for I had very little time to myself. While Jenny spent the days alone except for the company of fifteen pounds of baby, I was at work manning cash registers, making book recommendations, hearing creative reasons why employees could not make it to work. When I got home, Jenny either wanted meaningful conversation or she wanted me to take Afton off her hands. Fair or not, both of these options would occasionally piss me off. *When is we supposed to write*? Golem whispered in my ear. *When is we to go on our nice, long jogs-es*? When was I supposed to organize my life and point it in a meaningful direction?

The answer to those questions? 4:00 a.m.

No one is awake at 4:00 a.m. If you're up at that time, you can go for a run, you can write a thousand words, hell, you can watch a TV show that only you like (I never did that). So I started exercising hard in the mornings, running and following a serious regimen of pushups. I stopped submitting *The Mallards* to agents and began work on a new book. By the time I got to the store each morning, I had run four miles, done a hundred pushups, written a thousand words, and drunk three cups of coffee. I was bouncing off the walls. I was probably unbearable to be around.

After work, I was tired but not concerned about my time. Everything that Golem complained about I had given him before the sun rose. With my self-pity quelled I was free to fully engage with Jenny, play with the baby, be a decent person to the people I loved.

And it didn't stop. In the fall of 2011 I was studying for the GRE, writing a book on retainer, running countless miles, taking care of a baby, and working forty hours a week. I stumbled like a Saturday-night-drunk around the bookstore, completely exhausted but satisfied that shit was getting done.

A year and a half later, another novel finished, another failed attempt to sell the novel. Fuck it, start writing another.

And so it went.

Going into the coding boot camp, I knew I had a secret weapon: I can work really, really hard if I want to. The results of that work are suspect, maybe, but I can push.

And that's exactly what I had to do on the third day of class. I came in cocky, I'll admit it. I was two days in and I had no reason to think that the lesson on the third day would be any harder than the one on the first or second.

As far as the lesson was concerned, I was right. I comprehended, for the most part. It was the introduction of conditional logic and methods.

Conditional logic is easy enough to understand, and it is fundamental to the way in which computers work. A mathematician in the mid 1800s named George Boole created an algebraic system based entirely on answers being true or false. Every single answer to every single problem must be either true or false. Nothing else. This is called Boolean Algebra, and Boolean Algebra is the foundation of computer science. There is a type of variable used in all computer languages usually called bool or Boolean, and this variable's value must be either (you guessed it) true or false.

We've all heard of bytes, I think. If not, pull out your phone and look it up. A byte is a unit of information usually made up of eight bits. Think of a bit as a switch that can either be flipped in the "on" position or the "off "position. That's all the bit does. It switches on or it switches off.

Another thing that most people know about computer languages is that "it's all just ones and zeroes." Picture the green and black scroll from the *Matrix* movies. This is true. And it's true because of the bit. When the bit is in the on position, we call that "one" and when the bit is in the off position, we can call that "zero." In a computer chip, you flip the switch with an electric current, and in a hard drive it's done with magnetism, but the same result occurs. What was one is now zero. What was on is now off. What was true is now false. Boolean.

With these bits, one can write in binary, which is a computer language made up entirely of strings of ones and zeroes. This is the original language that all other computer languages are built upon. This is the language the computer "understands" because it communicates with the computer's very fiber—its bits.

The conditional logic that I was learning on the third day of Tech Elevator was way down the line from this low-level logic. But it was still Boolean.

As an example of what I was dealing with, here is a logic problem:

If Sean writes a book that is more than four hundred pages long, no one will read it. Also, no one will read the book if it is boring because he writes too much about confusing computer stuff.

Write a method that takes Sean's book and determines if people will read it.

Answer:

```
public bool WillBookBeRead(Book bookToRead)
{
  bool successfulBook;

  if (bookToRead.length > 400 &&
      bookToRead.sucks == false)
  {
    successfulBook = true;
  }
  else
  {
    successfulBook = false;
  }

  return successfulBook;
}
```

So let's go through this. First off, this is what we call a method. A lot of new programmers will write their code willy nilly in the main file, solving each problem as it comes. But this isn't efficient. You will come across the same problems over and over again and end up writing the same code over and over again. To solve this, you want a reusable block of code that solves a specific problem that you can plug into your code any time that problem arises. A method.

The method above determines whether a book will be read. The first line is called the signature. The first word "`public`" means the method can be accessed anywhere in the code base, "`bool`" is the variable type that the method will return as an answer, and "`WillBookBeRead`" is the method name. We can accept an instance of a class (an object) called "`Book`" in the constructor (the parentheses after the method name). We'll cover classes and objects later. If you wanted to use the method in your code, you would put a book in the constructor so that it would look like this:

```
WillBookBeRead(refactored)
```

Then "refactored" would go through the body of the method and be subject to its conditional logic. The next line is what is called an "if statement." In English, the code in the parentheses after "`if`" is saying "if the book length is less than four hundred and the book does not suck, then execute the code within the curly braces. If either of these things is not true, move on and do not execute the code in the curly braces."

So, if the book is under four hundred pages and it does not suck, the method will return "`successfulBook` is true." If either of these criteria is false—say the book is eight hundred pages or I continue writing about the theories of George Boole for the next six chapters—then the code within the parentheses after the "`if`" will be skipped and the code beneath will happen. In this case, the method will return "`successfulBook` is false."

So that's that.

Now, clearly, this method will not work accurately for all books. *Harry Potter and the Deathly Hallows*, coming in at 759 pages, would return unsuccessful. But it is one of the most successful books of all time. And *The End of the Affair* by Graham Green, passing all the criteria with 191 pages and a clear bool of `book.sucks == false`, is read by approximately one person every ten years worldwide.

But I suspect the method is valid for my book.

So, I understood Bill's lesson well enough. I got the parts of the method straight in my head, I understood variables as well as one can, and I took to conditional logic reasonably. Then I pulled the homework assignment down from the repository: thirty-five problems.

OK, I thought, *that's a lot, but I can do this.*

As I got going, I realized that any of these problems could take me between ten and thirty minutes. Doing some quick math in my head, it was clear that I was in for a marathon. *This must be the "boot camp" part*, we joked with each other, laughing nervously.

This is also the first time I was introduced to the unit test.

I read each question, did my best to satisfy all its demands by crafting a method, and then hit the "run test" button, which fed my method a series of test data, making sure that it was bulletproof and correct. The unit test took three to eight seconds to work, and when it was finished running, a line appeared at the top of the screen. If my method worked, the line was green and I could move on to the next problem. If the line was red, it had failed one or more of the unit tests and I had to debug, find the fault in my logic, bang my damn head against the wall until I got that line to turn green. I did some swearing.

The quickest students worked from 1:00 p.m. to approximately 6:00 p.m. The quickest students worked quietly and asked few, if any, questions. The quickest students packed up their computers and climbed into their coats, headed for home. This was the point when I realized I wasn't one of them. I had arrived at Tech Elevator at 7:00 a.m. and I finished the last of my logic problems at 7:30 p.m.

I felt high on the way home, my mind stretched out and numb. I probably shouldn't have been driving. I had felt this before, after working all day on a novel, lost in a world of my own design, spaced out and loopy when made to return to regular reality.

My thoughts were completely scattered after my herculean coding effort, but scattered with mostly positive things. I had done it. I had finished all thirty-five problems. Sure, there were some students who were better than me, faster than me, but there were others who weren't. Several budding programmers were still bowing over their white screens when I left, as if in prayer. Some of them, I would find out the next day, stayed until 10:00 p.m.

As I thought over some of the trickier questions on the drive home, I found comfort in the fact that I knew all of my work was correct. When I hit the run button, that green line appeared at the top of the screen indicating that all unit tests were happy, that my methods were good to go. After a day of working on a novel, all that you're left with are questions: Does this make sense for the character to say? Is the pacing too slow? Or too fast, maybe? Is this prose irredeemably shitty? There is no green line when you nail a solid metaphor, no red when you've left a gaping plot hole.

I smiled as I pulled my car into the garage. It was nice to know where I stood for once.

| Chapter Six |

I decided that I would sit in a new seat every day. I wanted to not only meet all the people in my class, but really get to know them. The best way to do that was to sit next to them.

There are three tables in the .NET classroom, each lined with monitors to plug laptops into. The other students at the table, and especially the person you're sitting next to, become allies in the battle against your homework. It is not only encouraged, but necessary to ask other students for help when attending Tech Elevator. There is only one Bill in each class and there were sixteen .NET students. In a class concerning Chemistry or English, that ratio might work, but with coding, one problem could sideline both student and teacher for over thirty minutes. You had to lean on the other people in class.

The first day, I sat next to Rob and we joined brains on the Git homework. The next day I sat at the middle table and met Brandon, a fast-talking former gym manager from Youngstown. After that I sat by Wayne and Diane and finally I sat next to Craig.

When I first met Craig, I found him standoffish. He was a little different than the rest of the .NET class in that he seemed like he might be cool. His jeans fit properly, he had a well-trimmed beard, a Dogfish Head Brewing hat, and obscure T-shirts, the references of which I sometimes did not understand. I found him standoffish, though admittedly, I often find people standoffish whom I suspect might be cooler than me. It's something of a defense mechanism.

As it turns out, Craig is a nerd, though not in the traditional sense. Yes, there are some bread-and-butter nerd qualities about him—the fact that he's built ten or more computers and his unabiding love for Magic the Gathering come to mind. But he's also into traditionally cool things too. He has a vast knowledge of indie and forgein films and suggested several movies that I had never heard of but were incredible. His taste in music is discerning and impressive—a deep understanding of not only the catalogues of the Rolling Stones and Bob Dylan, but also lesser known icons like Pavement and Tom Waits. He loves good food and is familiar with the hippest places to dine in Pittsburgh, which has a budding food scene that can be dizzying to keep up with.

I told Craig that I played guitar and he answered, "Oh, cool. I play a little too."

I had Craig over my house one night to play guitar and drink beers. He showed up with a suitcase full of pedals, an amp, and professional-level guitar skills. I hack around with chords on an acoustic guitar. Craig is a wiz, so much so that I have trouble keeping up. He played with local Pittsburgh rock bands post highschool and through college. When I thought-out-loud once to Craig that I never studied anything like I was currently studying code—ten to twelve hours a day when classwork, reading, and homework were combined, he agreed. Then he thought for a moment and said, "Well, I guess I used to practice guitar that much."

He's a super dork who is also cool and his super dorkiness bleeds into his cool interests. He likes Tom Waits, so he once wrote a college dissertation on one of Waits's albums. He's into guitar, but he wants to practice to the point where a doctor would probably prescribe medication to get him to stop. All-in-all, he's my kind of guy. I stopped jumping around the room after that first day that I sat next to Craig.

But not everyone found their spot as quickly as I did. The second day, the day that I was sitting next to Brandon, Matt stood up in the middle of Bill's lecture and moved to our table. Matt's eyes were wide and he was shaking his head.

Unlike the TE staff, Matt is not a large man. At five foot six and one hundred and sixty pounds, it's hard to believe he was a collegiate athlete. But it's true. He was a standout baseball player and caught for William and Jefferson College for four years. He has a very deep voice and it carries no matter how he tries to whisper.

"I can't sit next to him," he told Brandon and me, "I just can't do it."

He didn't have to say who he was talking about. Brandon and I knew. Matt was talking about Wayne.

Wayne, though one of the kindest-natured and well-intentioned men I've ever met, was a repeating source of stress in the .NET classroom. Wayne is an immigrant from Scotland. He's been in America for some years, but still carries a little bit of Robbie Coltrane's Hagrid character in his speech. He is deeply religious, but not pushy with his Christianity. He mentions it in conversation every now and then, but only because it's such a big part of his life. He wears shirts produced by his church, the best of which reads, "Jesus Saved Yinz." He, like several others in the cohort, is a workout enthusiast, to the point where the first thing you might think about him upon meeting is *that guy works out*. Jason, the chef of .NET, once declared Wayne the "most swole" person in the cohort. Fair enough.

Wayne asked a lot of questions. And that's fine. We *should* ask questions. Most times his questions were directed at Bill while he lectured, but sometimes they were to Rick who sat next to him. These questions were often directed at Matt until Matt ran away. When Wayne doesn't think anyone in his general vicinity might know the answer to his latest question, he might ask the open air, "Object? What's that mean? What's an Object? I don't get this stuff."

When Wayne *does* understand something, there is a steady stream of *Oohs* and *Aahs* as Bill continues the lecture. Wayne might mutter, "Oooooooh, so that's how that works." The commentary ran throughout most lectures.

When the homework was assigned, Wayne had the tendency to attach himself to another student and continue his stream of queries. The student-in-question started off not minding, not only because most people were earnestly willing to help out, but also because Wayne would stroke their vanity, often cooing, "Wow. How do you know all this?" When the student would tell Wayne that they had just, moments ago, learned it in Bill's lecture, or when they would point to the screen where it said in text exactly what they had just told Wayne, Wayne would shake his head and repeat again and again, like the chorus of a Daft Punk song, "I just don't get this stuff."

And, to be fair, I didn't get this stuff either. At least not on that sixth day of class. I often cite the Monday and Tuesday of that week as my worst days. We started learning how to build objects on the second Monday of the cohort. Objects, overall, I grasped. But the logic problems that went along with them nearly drove me insane.

So, remember the method from the last chapter? Here it is again:

```
public bool WillBookBeRead(Book bookToRead)
{
  bool successfulBook;

  if (bookToRead.length > 400 &&
      bookToRead.sucks == false)
  {
    successfulBook = true;
  }
  else
  {
    successfulBook = false;
  }

  return successfulBook;
}
```

If you recall, this method takes a book as a parameter and then gives a bool as a response indicating whether or not the book will be successful. One question the observant reader might have is, how does the method know how many pages the book has? How does the method know whether the book sucks or not? Good questions. I left that part out.

The `WillBookBeRead` method takes a book object as a parameter, meaning it is put within the parentheses after the method name. The book object had to be previously defined somewhere else in the code, in a sort of blueprint for the object called a "class." The class would look something like this:

```
public class Book {
  int length {get, set}
  bool sucks {get, set}
}
```

Here, we've defined a class called "book" that has two values—an integer called "`length`" and a bool called "`sucks`." An integer must be a whole number between -2147,483,648 and 2,147,483,648 and a bool, as we know, must be either true or false. Think of our class as an empty container that can be filled up with real data, so long as it adheres to the criteria we've laid out. When we fill that empty container up with actual data, then we have "instantiated" the class. To instantiate means that we create a representation of our class with real data. When we instantiate a class, we have created an "object." We can instantiate as many book objects as we please. Let's instantiate the book class with the book you're currently reading like so:

```
Book refactored = new Book();
refactored.length = 240;
refactored.sucks = false; (Right? I mean, you've
    read this far without ripping it in half...)
```

We've made an instance of the class book called "`refactored`" and we've given that instance a length value and a sucks value. It's now an object. We can feed it into our method and get an answer. This was the bones of the lesson that Bill taught us that day and, though it wasn't part of my pre-study, I followed along all right.

The problem was that the homework wasn't about objects. It was about manipulating strings. (Snippets of text, in the programming world are called "strings." It's a little more complicated than that, but for this book it will suffice. Strings are text.) This was only a small part of the lesson, but the lion's share of the homework. The reason for this is because manipulating strings can lead to complicated logic problems.

Now, instead of using conditional logic to solve some problem, we were given a run of words, told to take the middle two letters out of one word and then return the remaining letters of the word backwards. I stared at the first problem for a good ten minutes thinking to myself, "I just don't get this stuff." But I put my head down and started churning out methods.

The red line of failing unit tests haunted me until late into the evening. My head was pounding as I stared hard at the screen, the clock nearing 8:00 p.m., and the red line like a knife gash telling me that the method I wrote did not work.

"What the fuck," I said for the thirtieth time that day. "What. The. Fuck."

Craig had finished about an hour ago and I still had eleven of the thirty-five problems remaining. We worked on a couple problems together while he was still there, but it quickly became clear that he was much better at logic than I was. When our pair programming started to become a straight-up lesson from Craig to me, I backed off, saying, "All right. Cool. I'll figure it out."

I did this for three reasons. Firstly, I didn't want to make the mistakes that Wayne was making. Just like me, Craig had a lot of work to do. It was unfair to ask him to also be my tutor. Secondly, some of the help he was giving me I didn't understand. The unit test turned green, but I didn't know why. This was no good. I needed to learn how to solve these logic problems and what I was doing with Craig was tantamount to copying my homework. And the third reason, of course, was pride. But I didn't need to worry about that. My pride would soon be crushed into nonexistence.

The next morning I still had eleven problems to finish on the homework. It was Tuesday and the assignment wasn't due until Wednesday after the lecture. But, realistically, I knew I might receive between fifteen and forty new problems this afternoon. I couldn't let the stuff from Monday hang around. I arrived at seven in the morning with a plan of knocking out eight problems before the lecture started. That was four problems in each hour, totally doable.

I finished three problems altogether by the time that Bill told us to login to Socrative.

I didn't have a headache, per se, more of a buzzing of murderous rage sloshing around my brain. My face was tingling with frustration and I could feel my heart beating in the skin of my forehead. Technically, the day hadn't even started yet.

I made sure to calm myself down before the quiz. I took some deep breaths and plastered a fake smile on my face. But then I missed the second question on the quiz and became just as angry as I had been while working on the logic questions. I was a covered pot to which the smallest increase in heat would send water boiling over the sides. I missed the next question and the one after that. Craig craned his neck to look at me without turning his chair. I was slamming things around, muttering under my breath—basically acting like a baby. A baby who swears a lot.

I calmed down marginally and finished the quiz. Five out of twelve. Not good. Something needed to change.

Two groups had quickly formed in the .NET class: those who stayed in the classroom to do their homework and those who went out to the Elevate Space, the large room with the kitchen, couches, high top tables, ping pong, and rusty, large letters in the window, which read "ELEVATE." Those who stayed in the classroom didn't exactly work quietly, but they worked independently. They comprehended the lessons and preferred to solve the problems, for the most part, on their own. Those in the Elevate Space were there primarily because that's where Bill set up shop in the afternoon. The high top area became, in many ways, a discussion over the homework, solving problems together and wrangling Bill into the conversation when the collective got stuck. Left to its own devices, the .NET class had divided itself into advanced and remedial.

Until this point, I had stayed in the classroom. Not because my skill set allowed me to do so, but because I *wished* my skill set allowed me to do so. But the illusion had been dispelled. I had eight problems left from Monday's assignment and twelve more (a mercy) from Tuesday's. My exodus from the gifted class was required.

I sat next to Rob at the high top closest to the window. Wayne was at the table too, not getting stuff, and Rick sat just behind us. Rob, while not being the best natural coder, had quickly become known for a ridiculous work ethic. He worked slowly but he was tireless. He had not yet gone home without that day's assignment finished. I didn't witness it first hand, but it was said that he had stayed until eleven o'clock every night this week after arriving each morning at eight or nine. Those are some marathon days, and the warning of burnout followed Rob wherever he roamed.

Rob was a great person to work with, as was Rick. Rick, though sitting in the Elevate Space rather than the gifted class, was picking up the lessons like it was nothing. Rick is a solid, husky fellow, who surprised everyone some months into the cohort when he arrived at class wearing shorts that revealed his brightly tattooed legs. Upon first meeting Rick, he came off as reserved, quiet, and polite. Rick is an extremely thoughtful and kind person. During those early days of class, he had the conversational tone of a saint or Mr. Rogers or Barack Obama. Just *really* kind, *really* smart, and *completely* willing to help you out. The reason he was in the

Elevate Space and not in the gifted class is because he knew that people would need his help and he was utterly willing to give it.

But as the months grew on, his obscured personality became clearer. He began making clever jokes, showed a deep knowledge and love of exotic foods, became heatedly competitive over ping pong, and started riding his motorcycle to class on warmer days, carrying a hyper-color helmet that matched his tattoos perfectly.

Once, when asked in the general public of the kitchenette what he was doing this weekend, he calmly replied, “I don’t know. I think my girlfriend and I might eat acid.”

Some weeks into the cohort, Rick raised his hand during a lecture and asked Bill if a certain method could be written a different way. Bill looked at his work on the white board for a moment, chewing on his lower lip.

“Groovy,” Bill muttered to himself.

He moved over to a clear space and rewrote the method following Rick’s suggestion. While Bill was writing, he said, “So, if you want to do it the *Rick Fancy* way, we could write it like this.”

That stuck. From then on, Rick was known as Rick Fancy, or just Fancy for short. He seemed to like being called that.

Soon, Wayne had gone to ask Bill a question about one of the problems and Rob, Fancy, and I plowed through the work together. Like in the gifted class, we worked quietly for the most part, but each of us in turn would sometimes mutter a question. Often, someone in our trio would have figured it out already and throw out the answer, but sometimes we could gather around the questioner’s computer, the white glow illuminating our curious expressions, as we worked our way toward green lines.

| Chapter Seven |

MY morning routine changed some because of Tech Elevator. I did not set the alarm for four in the morning while attending the boot camp. It wasn't laziness, but a strategic decision. I pay a price when getting up at four in the morning. Yes, I get my exercise and writing done consistently, but when I was working at Barnes & Noble and later at Green Basil, this schedule caused me to space out in the afternoons. My energy level in the morning was near manic, but after lunch I crashed.

Back then, I was fine with crashing. I didn't need to be fully awake to do my job well. I was pleased with my writing progress, my health, and my mental attitude toward family time—if I felt a little drowsy in the afternoons, well, I call that a fair trade.

But that wouldn't do for the intensive boot camp. I needed to refactor my energy so that it was going 100 percent toward learning to code. I pushed the alarm back to 5:00 a.m. That way, if I got to bed by nine or ten, I was still getting between seven and eight hours of sleep. I altered my exercise. In the summer I'm all about running outside, but in the winter, I usually do hard cardio either on the treadmill or through heavy bag workouts that I follow on YouTube (HasFit!). But I've found that doing cardio exercise can also make me spacey. Instead, I only ran one mile in the mornings at a leisurely pace and then lifted weights. I've always found that if you're looking for mental clarity, anaerobic exercise has it all over cardio.

After my exercise, I participated in the great meditation experiment. I had attempted meditating maybe a half a dozen times before, but never found it very useful. After the second Monday of Tech Elevator, I knew I needed something to deal with the stress. I started meditating the following day and I felt better. I'm not sure it was the mediating that made me feel better. It's possible that I had hit rock bottom when I was flipping out over the failing unit tests and was slowly on my way back up. But I couldn't be sure it *wasn't* the meditation that was heightening my mood. I kept up the practice throughout the duration of the cohort just in case.

Sweaty from the run and arms tingling from lifting, I turned off the lights and sat cross-legged on the mildewy floor of my basement. I set a timer on my phone for ten minutes. Then, I counted to ten over and over again in my head—one, breath in, one, breath out, two breath in, two breath out. I tried to think of nothing but the inhales and exhales. When I reached the count of ten I started over.

I never, ever, *ever* got to ten without my mind wandering. Right around six or seven, I would think about some problem from the homework, something Afton said the day before, the plotline of the book I was reading, some stupid memory from years past that had no business being in my head. Then I would think—stop! Stop! Stop! Back on the count. Concentrate on the count. Honestly, I found meditating kind of stressful. Still, I did it for four solid months.

But if my morning routine seems odd, there were other students that were doing crazier things.

Take Brandon, for instance. He was driving from Youngstown, Ohio to Pittsburgh every day for class. And he was also driving back home at night, often not getting on the road till seven or eight. For those of you unfamiliar with the Ohio/Pennsylvania/West Virginia tri-state area, that's over three hours of driving a day. Add to that four hours of class, two hours of the Pathway program and six hours of homework and that leaves very little time for things like sleep or eating, let alone maintaining a relationship with his girlfriend or family.

But he was doing it. He had one cup of coffee right when he woke up, listened to podcasts on his hour and a half drive in, and another three cups of the strong joe provided by TE once he arrived. Brandon eats very little and talks very fast. The coffee only exacerbated his cadence. By the time he was told to take his Socrative survey, he had to truthfully answer that his energy level was nearing a ka-billion.

He never seemed to slow down. Now and then, when speaking with Brandon, he'll get a spacey look in his eye. I used to assume he was distracted and thinking about something else, but maybe he was taking micro-naps.

I found out about Brandon's commute toward the end of the second week of class.

"If you ever need to crash, just let me know," I told him. "I live ten minutes from here."

"Really?" Brandon asked.

"Yeah, definitely," I said.

"Would I be able to tonight?"

"Sure," I said, immediately thinking I should have probably asked Jenny about this first.

I gave Brandon my cell number and address around six o'clock as we were finishing up our homework. He typed the address into his phone for directions and I drove home the way I always drive home. There was an accident on the West End Bridge and I hit some really awful traffic. Brandon's phone had foreseen this traffic and rerouted him around the mess. As I sat on the bridge, my radio turned off, I began to get anxious.

Firstly, I didn't want Jenny to have to entertain someone she had never met before while they waited who-knows-how-long for me to show up and be the conduit for conversation. I also didn't want Brandon, who was a few years younger than me, to show up at my place and have me not be there, have to introduce himself and make conversation with my eight-year-old who wouldn't know what the hell was going on. And lastly, even with these minor awkwardnesses aside, I was letting someone I didn't know at all sleep in my house. Like I said, Brandon was younger than me, but he was also a lot bigger than me and, having worked in a gym for much of his life, a lot stronger. What if he was some maniac, some dangerous thug from Youngstown, who had enrolled in Tech Elevator just to worm his way into a fellow student's home and murder their entire family so he could steal all the books and musical instruments he could get his hands on?

Luckily, this wasn't the case.

Brandon made the decision I probably would have made—he stayed in his car until I arrived. Smart man.

When we entered my house, we found that Jenny had made a taco dinner. We sat down to eat, spooning mounds of pork, chorizo, guacamole, and diced tomatoes onto our corn tortillas. Brandon sipped a beer and politely asked Jenny about her career and where she was from (Jenny is also an Ohioan). He made conversation with Afton—just simple stuff about what grade she was in and how old she was. When the conversation came around to Brandon, however, he tended to deflect anything personal and talk instead about the experience we were currently sharing, our time at Tech Elevator, the crew of big personalities in our class.

It took me nearly a year to learn that Brandon was actually from Warren, a suburb of Youngstown. He had worked at a gym, but had also spent a good amount of time at IT jobs, so some of the things we were seeing at TE weren't completely new to him. The Youngstown area isn't exactly known for its education, with only 13 percent of adults over age twenty-five having a bachelor's degree or higher, but Brandon and his girlfriend Ashley are the exception. Warren, OH where Brandon went to school, was decent, but Ashley had it rough. She attended Chaney High School, which in 2017 ranked in the bottom 5 percent of Ohioan schools with a 919th statewide ranking. According to Brandon, there were eight hundred students in her class and only one hundred graduated. Despite this, Ashley went on to earn a doctorate in physical therapy, one of only two students to ever earn a doctorate after graduating from Chaney.

Ashley had encouraged Brandon to attend Tech Elevator. She told him about it on Christmas day of 2018, Brandon applied on January 3, and on the nineteenth of that same month, he showed up for his first day of class.

Brandon and I still had to read our material for the next day's lesson, so after dinner we remained at the table and cracked a second beer as we scrolled our computer screens for the tenth or eleventh hour that day.

Halfway through the second beer, the computer screens closed, material left unread. There was too much to talk about. We were too excited about things. What would we know about coding when we finally graduated? Who from the class might have the most success in interviews? And, of course, money. One of the many things I like about Brandon, he doesn't mind talking about money one bit.

Once, a friend of mine, a British fellow named Adam with a successful track record of starting his own businesses, besmirched a mutual acquaintance by saying, "He always wants to talk about money. The only people who want to talk about money are those who don't have it."

That might be true. It was also true that Adam said this to a man who made less than eighteen dollars an hour. I *love* talking about money. And so does Brandon. Because we've never really had that much of it. We're like two fourteen-year-olds talking about sex.

In 2019, Tech Elevator had a placement rate of 92 percent within six months of graduating from their program. And those 92 percent of students made an average of $58,000 annually. Those numbers represented the TE programs in Cincinnati, Cleveland, Columbus, and Pittsburgh combined. It was said, though not official, that of the two classes that preceded us in the Pittsburgh market, only one student did not yet have a job and that student had (unthinkably) turned down several positions while he held out for the one he wanted. Also, the Pittsburgh market paid more. It was said that one could expect near $60,000 as a salary.

"Could you imagine making sixty thousand dollars?" I asked Brandon over our third beer.

"Dude, I couldn't imagine making *fifty* thousand dollars," he said.

"Me either," I agreed. "I would buy myself new clothes. My dress clothes have holes in them."

"You know what I'm going to do?" Brandon said. I always spoke about my future employment conditionally; Brandon liked to talk about it like it was a foregone conclusion. "After I get my first paycheck, I'm going to get a stack of ones and walk into the dollar store with a bunch of people and just buy anything. Just, like, *anything*."

"Yeah," I agreed, misty-eyed.

These were our dreams.

It snowed that night and was icy the next day. When I went down to exercise at five in the morning, Brandon was already up, dressed, looking at his phone. I think he slept, but I don't have any hard proof.

"Thanks for letting me stay," he said, looking out the window. "This would have been a terrible drive."

Brandon opened his computer and read the material from the night before while I ran on the treadmill. He washed up in the bathroom while I lifted weights. He paced around while I meditated below, the creaking of the floorboards under his weight disrupting my count. But I couldn't concentrate anyway. I couldn't even make it to three breaths before thinking about Youngstown, about jobs and code, and most of all, about money.

| Chapter Eight |

BACK in Caitie Zajko Land, the season of the Elevator Pitch was upon us. An elevator pitch, if you don't know, is a term borrowed from Hollywood. The idea is that if you find yourself in an elevator with an executive, you should be able to pitch your movie before you get to the lobby. Caitie wanted us to have a similar pitch prepared so that we could use them at the many networking events she demanded we attend.

She expected us to spend no small amount of time writing these things. First, Caitie had a demonstration where she broke down the different parts of the elevator pitch, sentence by sentence. There was a purpose to each and every line. She showed us video recordings of former TE students standing in their own living rooms in front of their phones and computers, awkwardly describing themselves and their passions. Everyone used the word "passion," without exception.

After the presentation, we had some quiet time in which to begin our first draft. Admittedly, I scribbled something down and then slinked back to the classroom to try and chip away at my mountain of homework.

Feeling guilty over this half-assing, I made sure to attend the optional workshop for the elevator pitch some days later. Eight other people attended the workshop, and we squeezed into a small, gray office, each clutching our self-made scripts while Caitie looked on, wearing an expectant smile.

Kane, a tall, beefy kid from the country towns south of Pittsburgh went first. If let loose, Kane's hair fell past his shoulders, but he always kept it in a neat bun. He wore delicate glasses, which he would occasionally remove with one of his tattooed arms to rub his bloodshot eyes. Before Tech Elevator, Kane had spent his time split between a bar, where he worked serving drinks, and gyms, where he trained as a boxer. Being an avid combat sports fan, I was sort of fascinated by him and would goad him into talking about the sweet science when I could muster the courage.

I arrived at TE early every morning, but Kane was always there before me, set up in a side office, sipping coffee. If you asked him how it was going, he reliably replied, "Livin' the dream, Sean. Livin' the dream." If you asked again because you didn't want to accept the canned answer, he would calmly explain that he didn't understand why he wasn't getting better at coding. If he spent this much time training to box, he would kill his training partners. Literally kill them.

I didn't know much else about Kane, but it didn't surprise me to learn as he read his elevator pitch that he came from poverty. His demeanor revealed someone who had known hardship enough that it was commonplace. He had never met his father and felt that he owed his mother a great debt. The gist of his elevator pitch was that he wanted to learn to be a software engineer so that he could support his mother who had supported him for so many years.

Now, I admit, the pitch pulled on the heart strings. However, Kane, charismatic but not accustomed to public speaking, really butchered the delivery. The writing could be juiced up too. The pitch would end up being solid, I thought, it had soul, but he needed to put in some work. Keep the plot, but scrap everything else.

Caitie disagreed. She was over the moon. She loved how personal it was and thought it captured his plight perfectly.

Fine. Not wanting to seem like an asshole, I withheld my critiques.

I went next. Here is what I had written:

> Hi, I'm Sean and I'm a .NET student at Tech Elevator. In my first career, I was a manager at Barnes & Noble. I was in charge of making schedules, hiring, and planning merchandise reorganizations.
>
> Barnes & Noble was a good fit— not only because I like to read, but also because I've personally written several novels.
>
> But even though I was surrounded by books, the job did not challenge me creatively. My ability to look forward and plan creatively is my greatest strength. Through Tech Elevator, I've found that coding allows me to utilize this strength every single day.
>
> I'm looking for a Junior Software Developer position where I can creatively contribute to a team and where I can continue to grow as a programmer.

Perfect? Certainly not. I didn't think it was. A solid jumping off point, though.

"Wow," Caitie said. "Just...wow. Am I going to have to do *anything* in this workshop?"

She looked from Kane to me like we were Hemingway and Fitzgerald. Kane is clearly the Hemingway.

"Geez," she said, shaking her head. "Let's keep it going."

There eventually were pitches that we needed to fix. There were a few students speaking English as a second language who wanted help with grammar issues and there were those who simply could not construct a coherent narrative, no matter the language. I was a little leary of my elevator pitch, but with Caitie's enthusiasm for it, I didn't change a thing. What you see written above ended up being the finished product.

So what did we use these things for? Well, there was one utility that I put it to often, and that was in personal conversations with working professionals. Anytime anyone working in software heard that I was in a coding boot camp, they eventually asked, "What did you do before?"

I didn't deliver the pitch verbatim in these situations. There were students who, to my utter horror, did exactly this. Someone would say, "What did you do before this program" or "Tell me about yourself" or "Hi" and it was like a string was pulled on the Chatty Cathy doll. "My name is Daniel and I'm a student at Tech Elevator." It was the opposite of networking.

I delivered my elevator pitch piecemeal, in a conversational way, like a human would do. I found it useful to have this blurb memorized. Having practiced it, I was able to access the information without too much thought. I feel like I came off sensible and prepared in conversations with potential employers.

But there was another use for the elevator pitch that I didn't much care for. Caitie had scheduled a steady parade of software professionals to come through TE and speak with the class. Some of these professionals would sit on panels, Caitie moderating them through a series of questions about the interviewing process, day-to-day-life at a software company, jobs that are coding adjacent, like the emerging DevOps movement. Then, there were the showcases. A company who was interested in hiring TE grads would send two or three representatives, buy us all lunch, and then give a pitch as to why we should work there. These presentations are a major part of the Pathway program and they are indispensable to the TE experience.

What is dispensable is leading off these presentations with our elevator pitches.

The visitors, be they speakers or representatives of a hiring company, stood politely at the head of the Elevate Space and tried their damnedest to keep the cringe off their faces as we stood, one-by-one, to deliver our elevator pitches.

"Hi, I'm Stephen and I'm a Java student at Tech Elevator. Before taking this program, I was a manager at Whole Foods..."

"Hi, I'm Diane and I'm a .NET student at Tech Elevator. I used to be a personal trainer and run my own business and now..."

"Hi, I'm Jimmy. Not only am I a Java student at Tech Elevator, but I'm also a proud father of two..."

"Hi, I'm Sean and I'm a .NET student at Tech Elevator. Please don't shoot yourself before I finish speaking..."

It was terrible.

The worst time we delivered our elevator pitches was to a live audience during a field trip. We had a half day at the House of Metal and then drove out to Reynolds Sportswear corporate headquarters in Coraopolis. (This is pronounced "core-E-aw-poe-liss."

The pronunciation makes no sense. It is a linguistic abomination that could only be conceived in southwestern Pennsylvania.)

Coraopolis is far outside of Pittsburgh. From the North Side, it is more than a half-hour drive, or, as the locals would tell you, "Aht near tha airport." Many of the students in the class lived on the East End of Pittsburgh, making the commute more than an hour when traffic is considered.

To compensate for being in the middle of nowhere, Reynolds has put together a fantastic set of office buildings. Their workspace looks more like a college campus than an office building. The lobby is reminiscent of a pricey hotel, except sports-themed. There are comfortable leather chairs to sit in, Reynolds logos on everything, murals hanging overhead of muscular swimmers, men loping over hurdles, running on deep red racing tracks.

The tour sort of blew my mind. The ceilings in the lobby were at least fifty thousand feet high. When we got past security and into the real office, it was dotted with ping pong tables and cafeterias. There was a Starbucks. There was a legitimately nice restaurant where you could get a steak. Out the windows, in the cold winter air, were basketball and tennis courts waiting for the spring when they would be filled with bouncing balls.

And in every nook and cranny of this establishment were people crouched behind computers, typing away, writing code. It was the first time I had seen software developers in the wild. There were giant mounted screens where several developers gathered round and debated the obscure writing, hyper-color, graffiti in an alien script.

We followed our guide into an auditorium where one of the company's higher-ups was set to speak. Tech Elevator had its own section of seats and as we waited, packs of employees strolled in and found seats far away from us. They were young, these employees, and way better looking than the software developers and business people we had met at other companies. There were athletic clothes, clean haircuts, and definitely some flirting going on a few rows up.

The speaker walked out to a smattering of applause and led off by saying he really hated talking about himself. He then talked about himself for an hour and twenty minutes—which was twenty minutes over the allotted time of his speech. He had me captivated at the beginning. Though, admittedly, I think I *wanted* to be captivated because I already liked the cushy corporate headquarters and because I wanted a job literally anywhere. But as one story of his wiley, unconventional cunning bled into the next, I started to watch the clock on the wall. By the time his speech was ten minutes over its scheduled hour, the appreciative smile had faded from my face. By the time he finally stopped, I wasn't even listening any more. I don't think anyone was.

But it wasn't just the braggadocious speech that turned everyone off. It was also the fact that we had to deliver our elevator pitches afterwards. And as this higher-up from Reynolds rambled on and on, he was not only boring the entire room, he was extending our pain of anticipation.

Everyone breathed a sigh of relief when he finished and the room cleared of Reynolds employees, save those who were giving us the tour. There was some worry that we would deliver our pitches to the hundreds of people who had shown up for the speech. Luckily it was only to four Reynolds employees, two of which were Tech Elevator grads.

I did not like delivering my elevator pitch, but there were few, I suspect, who hated it worse than Christopher. Christopher is a very small man—maybe five foot two. He dressed in black almost all the time and often told stories of the tall men he dated—one, he claimed, was a seven-footer. Christopher had pulled Caitie aside and asked if he could go first with his elevator pitch. He was dealing with some anxiety and just wanted to get it out of the way. Christopher once asked me what I thought about the manner in which we deliver our elevator pitches. I said, "I don't think that if you have a good pitch it makes a difference. However, if you have a bad pitch, it does. So the elevator pitches seem like a chance to mess up your first introduction to an employer with no upside."

Looking back, I doubt my answer helped with Christopher's nerves.

I don't know that any of my fellow students agreed with my assessment, really. Some of them certainly thought that if they could nail the pitch it might make a good impression or even land them an interview. But all of them, myself included, looked upon the performance as a source of embarrassment.

Did I consider bringing my complaints to Caitie, as she was the driving force behind the creation and delivery of the elevator pitches? No, I didn't. Because public embarrassment does not register with Caitie Zajko. It is not something she fears. To Caitie, saying that you're embarrassed is like saying that you're afraid of vampires or the abominable snowman. It's kid's stuff.

Case in point: When we had our first Pathway meeting about our résumés, Caitie implored us all to take our seats and quiet down. It was time for her Résumé Rap, she said.

Yes, Résumé Rap.

Not realizing the gravity of the situation, Craig and I took our normal seats in the front, chuckling at what Caitie had said.

"So, D.J. Caitie's going to rap?" I asked Craig.

"I guess so," Craig laughed. "Hey, Caitie—you want me to beatbox for you?"

"No," Caitie said, like an aunt whose nephew has said something silly and adorable, "I have a beat recorded."

And she did. And she played it.

It was pretty old school, the beat—think Run DMC or the early Beastie Boys. Craig looked at me as Caitie retrieved a lyrics sheet from her podium.

"Wait, is she *really* going to rap?" he murmured.

"No," I said, half belief and half prayer.

In one hand, Caitie gripped the lyrics she had written. The other was held aloft as if suggesting that we all should perhaps raise the roof. Craig's jaw dropped and he stared aghast. I desperately wanted to leave the room. Many students bit their fists or covered their eyes. For the next minute and a half, Caitie spit lyrics. Here they are, verbatim[1]:

Ladies and gents, wanna hear a true story?

Saturday night, I was in my own glory.

They had CEOs linin' all up, ten local companies all hiring, that's wassup!

Took one manager aside wit me, his name was Thomas,

He was a yinzer[2] just like me.

He said, look at you tech enthusiast

A whole lots changed since I seen you last!

What would you do if you had no résumé?

[1]All slang spellings and questionable rhyme schemes are the work of the artist.

[2]A yinzer is a term, sometimes derogatory, used to describe a local resident of Pittsburgh.

Experience, not sure how to make it serious?

And the only way to make it.

Is your passion, motivation and your grit.

Add some tech experience, and get those dates in check.

Lots of hard work, and 14 weeks later, and now you're someone greater.

Now you have a résumé, and for me, this is now job history.

Not only did Caitie put on this rap show for the students of Cohort[2], she posted a video of it on LinkedIn. With this celebrated performance as evidence, it was clear that Caitie wasn't about to take pity on us if we claimed any degree of embarrassment concerning the elevator pitches. Get your ass to the front of the auditorium and say your damn pitch. To be clear, Caitie would never say this. It would be a sweet but firm insistence that you get your ass to the front of the auditorium and say your damn pitch.

And we did. We filed to the front few rows as the four representatives of Reynolds Sportswear smiled painfully. As planned, Christopher went first. He did really well. I sat next to Craig. (I always sat next to Craig. We were ride-or-die.) I went before him, tried not to act nervous, and just started speaking. Now, I admit, I'm not scared to speak in front of people. I was scared of this specific instance, because it seemed so manufactured and fake, but once I got going, I flowed all right.

On the way back to my seat, Craig gave me a withering look, as if by speaking well I had betrayed him. He gave his pitch right after me, worried and wringing his hands. He did fine. Craig spoke way better than he thought he spoke. Plus, he had what I could never successfully fake—he was actually a computer nerd.

There was a demonstration from the Reynolds employees after the elevator pitches. The Tech Elevator grads led it and, unfortunately, there were a lot of hiccups. They were trying to demonstrate a pipeline, a tech term I had never heard before. The pipeline kept getting stuck at one of the stages and the explanation of why it was getting stuck was unclear.

Next, there was a panel of four senior Reynolds employees. They talked about their journey through tech and what they did, day-to-day, at the company. Some of it was inspiring, some of it seemed contrived and forced. Really wanting to like the place, I ate it up, regardless of the content.

Finally, we had a short speech from a recruiter, the main idea of which was that we should be patient when we were interviewing with them because it might take a long time for them to get back to us. At one point, she checked her phone and then looked up at the other recruiter who was giving us the tour. "You know what? I have to go. I have a meeting in, like, five minutes."

"That's fine," the other recruiter said. (Male, by the way. Yes, it matters.)

As she walked up the steps, the male recruiter said, "And will you look at those pants? Aren't those something?"

The female recruiter was wearing high-waisted pants. The kind you would have called "mom jeans" in the '90s but are now back in style. She stopped on the stairs, holding her phone, and shot the male recruiter a glare. There was some nervous laughing from the TE group, but otherwise confused silence. You could hear the second hand tick on the clock.

There was some awkwardness, but then the male recruiter started talking again, describing what the interview process would be like and we all put our game faces back on.

Shuffling to the lobby, I was sold. Yes, the presentation was kind of strange, but the gym, the restaurants, the cool workspaces—this stuff added up. It wasn't my first choice, but perhaps a solid two or three. I was surprised to find out that not everyone was with me.

Back in the lobby, surrounded by sporty murals, I spoke with Christopher.

"I'm not even going to apply," he said.

"Why not?" I asked. "They have a gym."

"I don't give a fuck."

"Why don't you want to work here?"

He looked at me incredulously, like I didn't understand something fundamental.

"I would not fit in," he said.

It wasn't the fact that Christopher was gay that made him feel this way. He did, when questioned, feel that Reynolds was a very heterosexual company, a very straight company. College-fraternity-like. But he didn't specifically feel threatened by this. No, it was something else, something essential about Christopher. He was different. Different in a way that was hard to put your finger on. He spoke with a poetic cadence and a verbose vocabulary. He dressed like he was in mourning most of the time, never drank alcohol, and had a tendency to talk of incredibly personal things, often expecting reciprocation. He was right, he *wouldn't* fit in at Reynolds Sportswear.

The scene we had witnessed between the two recruiters certainly bolstered Christopher's opinion about the work environment at Reynolds. In the forefront of my mind now was the strange back-and-forth between the two recruiters, the man asking an entire auditorium of people to look at the lower half of a woman colleague. She was at work, busy, heading to a meeting, and he was imploring us to look at her pants as she walked away. It was objectification. It was harassment. Maybe one could consider it mild harassment, I don't know. But as I started thinking of all the masculine micro-cues of the day, a certain picture of the Reynolds culture began to emerge in my mind.

No, Christopher wouldn't fit in here, and the more I thought about it, the more it seemed like maybe I wouldn't either.

| Chapter Nine |

DANIEL was a teacher at Tech Elevator but did not have a class of his own during our cohort. Unlike the other behemoths working at TE, Daniel was of average height, with brown hair and a naturally friendly face. He seemed, more than the other two teachers, to embody the classic computer nerd tropes that one might expect of a boot camp teacher. The man's wedding cake had had code scrawled on the side in royal icing. He had taught in the first Java cohort, and during the second cohort he taught the inaugural .NET class while training Bill Reeves. Now, with Bill as a full-fledged teacher, Daniel helped out a bit with student questions but was mostly traveling around expanding the business of Tech Elevator, giving brief boot camps at various companies around the northeastern United States.

But today, he was in-person to deliver a career talk. He ran a short slide show about different paths we could take over the course of three, five, and ten years. There was the straight development path that went from junior to senior developer, there was the management path, which saw you eventually step back from coding and manage a team of coders, and there was the coding adjacent jobs, such as QA engineer, scrum master, and project manager.

Since everyone was in a coding boot camp, the most popular path in our imaginations was the development path. Daniel nodded, understanding this, but then warned, "Yeah, staying in straight development is good and all, but I have to tell you that at most companies, a senior dev is going to max out at ninety or a hundred thousand."

Craig and I looked at each other, side-eyed.

"Um, yes please," Craig said.

I think that $90,000 a year is a good salary to almost anyone. I realize that people working in a business setting might see salaries in and around this range all the time. But remember, I was making eighteen dollars a fucking hour. That's $36,000 a year. Much less than that, actually, when you consider that I was paying a lot of money for really terrible health care. I know that there are people making way less than $36,000 a year, and I'm not disparaging them or their tribulations. But those people know that if you make under $40,000 a year in America, bills can get out of control in a hurry.

When I first talked to Caitie, she had asked me what salary I would like to make.

"Um, I don't know, fifty?" I said.

That was my pie-in-the-sky-number.

Caitie set her pen down on top of her notebook and looked me in the eye.

"I think we can do much better than that," she said.

"Well, all right," I acquiesced. "But fifty would be fine."

And I meant it. Honestly, if I retired twenty-five years from now making $50,000, I would be totally satisfied with that and feel like a financial success. Fifty thousand dollars would be enough. But here in front of me, Daniel was saying that as a developer, we could expect to start near $60,000, make $70,000 to $80,000 within five years, and nearly $100,000 within a decade? Come on. I couldn't even imagine that kind of money. The things I'd always wanted to do—learn a martial art, take banjo lessons, travel extensively—that have been out of my reach because of my financial limitations—these things surfaced in my head one after the other in a series of daydreams.

There were plenty of other things that Daniel talked to us about, but, as I said before, I love talking about money. So I fixated on that and sort of drifted away, zoned out, and missed some of the other subjects he touched upon.

When I came to, it was question-and-answer time. Daniel was frank in this discussion.

"I know that in your elevator pitches, everyone talks about their *passion* for coding and no one talks about wanting to make more money. But, look, I'm not going to be your employer. Ask me any little thing your heart desires."

Many more questions about money followed. But it also became clear that a contingent of students joined the boot camp with the intention of working remotely. There were two or three questions of this ilk in a row.

"I have to say," Daniel winced, "that I wouldn't recommend taking a fully remote job as your first position. You're just not going to have the skill level to work by yourself like that. I strongly recommend landing somewhere with a team."

But the questions about working remotely continued. There were two or three students clearly having their bubbles burst over this.

"The first capstone is coming up," Daniel said. "You'll see. You'll see what it's like to work on a project and I think you'll come to realize that you're going to want people to lean on."

Capstone was a word I was not familiar with before attending Tech Elevator. A capstone, in educational terms, is the final lesson of a course or section of learning, integrating aspects of a class into a major project. There were no capstones required for my English degree. There would be three during our cohort and the first was just around the corner.

Though theoretically the nature of the assignment should have been a surprise, Bill had been tipping us off since the first day of class. We were going to create a digital vending machine. Each time Bill demonstrated some elegant strategy to approach a common problem he would stop writing on the board, turn his head and say, "This might be good to remember if you were to make, oh, I don't know, say...a *vending machine*?" Then he would continue with the lesson.

Maybe I should have been taking notes every time he said this but I didn't. There was too much to keep up with as it was, I didn't have the energy to look ahead and create a cheat sheet.

The teams for the first capstone were assigned randomly. I really didn't care whom I was paired with. Sure, it would be fun to work with Craig, but I felt confident about creating the vending machine, so much so that I thought I could do it myself. This was a foolish notion.

I was paired up with Arjun, a young man from Queens, New York, who actually sat next to me every day, on the opposite side from Craig. Arjun talked quickly and was fond of philosophy. He often carried a joyful expression on his face, even when frustrated. When he remembered to, he wore contact lenses, but he usually perched thick glasses on his nose. He kept his black hair quaffed in a large wave atop his head.

I wasn't sure how good Arjun was at coding, but he had the habit of writing to people on our chat channel, asking for methods to help with the homework that he couldn't figure out. I just sent the code, but Craig refused, ignoring his messages.

The vending machine was a command line application. This means that the front end, the part the customer sees and interacts with, is just white text on a black background. Our study so far had been all about Object Oriented Programming, which is essentially a back end-based theory of architecture. We had not studied HTML or CSS, which are the essentials of building a traditional-looking website. So, no, what we were building would not be a graphic depiction of a vending machine that lets one purchase food by clicking on it. The goal was to have a menu with the food items, the ability to select those items through entering a series of letters and numbers, and the ability to pay and then receive change. All of this would be in writing, not pictures.

We were given a text file that contained names, prices, and types of food. Instead of accessing a database (we had not yet studied databases), we were to feed this file into our software and use the data from the file in our vending machine.

Arjun and I talked it over, drew out some architectural plans the way that Bill had shown us, and then set to work. The first thing that we needed to do was import the data from the text file. We had never done this before. We tried one way, we tried another.

Suddenly, four hours had passed.

And this, Arjun and I were learning, is how coding goes. You think you have a handle on the project. You think you have a good plan. You think you'll finish in one work day. Then a small bump trips you for eight or nine solid hours.

We eventually sought out help from Daniel who showed us the error in our ways with our importing code. Happy with finally having the data, we started flying. Our fingers were a blur as we made a dozen classes, different methods, even an interface! Each time we had successfully figured out a problem that had slowed us down, Arjun looked up from his computer, turned to me with a serious demeanor, so out of place on his normally joyous face, and shook my hand. Then he cackled like Beavis and went back to his code.

We were feeling pretty good about ourselves as the clock passed five. Talk of finishing the next day and other wild delusions of grandeur were passed between us.

We packed up around six. As I was throwing my backpack across my shoulders I overheard the two wiz kids, Drew and Jack, talking about the day's work.

"Dude, did you see it, though?" Drew asked.

"Nooooo," sang Jack.

"They had, like, twelve different classes."

"Whaaaaaa?!"

"Yeah, like, one for each different food type. They wrote the same thing over and over again twelve times!"

"Duuuude!"

I knew they weren't talking about Arjun and me because they hadn't seen our code. But we had, just like the group they were talking about, made a class for each of the different food types. It seemed repetitive at the time, but I didn't stop to think. We had been so far behind because of the importing issue that writing simple code as fast as we could seemed like the right thing to do. Listening to Drew, I realized that we had forgotten one of the pillars of Object Oriented Programming: Inheritance.

There are three pillars of Object Oriented Programming and if you learn anything coming out of Tech Elevator, you will learn this. There is Encapsulation, abstracting our code out of the main file and calling methods rather than writing everything on top of each other. Polymorphism, using the ability of functions in different ways depending on the data type or class of their subject. And Inheritance, the ability of classes to take on the properties of a super class.

So here's the situation: there were to be three different types of gum in our vending machine. In our thoughtless dash, Arjun and I had made a class for each, giving each gum a name, a price, and so on. We did this three times, writing nearly the exact same code over again for each different type of gum. What we should have done was make an abstract "gum" class that was never instantiated. Then each type of gum inherits from this abstract class and we don't have to write the code again and again. That would have been the right and efficient way to do it.

On the drive home our mistake became clearer to me. All the foods from the files were in threes. Three different types of chips, three different chocolate bars, three different sodas. This challenge had clearly been designed to be met and solved by inheritance, and Arjun and I missed it. In trying to hurry we had wasted a ton of time.

The next morning we had a meeting with Bill to talk about the first day of capstone work. I gritted my teeth as he scrolled through our main file.

"Soooooo...there's not much *object orientation* going on with your programming, is there?"

I turned red. He had seen it right away.

"Yeah, we should have made a super class for the food types," I agreed. I looked at Arjun. "Maybe we should go back and fix that this morning."

While Arjun was nodding, Bill continued to scroll.

"Yeah, but it's not just that. I mean, you have allllllll this stuff in your main file." He pointed to a section on the three-hundredth line of our main file. "What does this do?"

"That's the method that accepts the money," I said.

"OK...," Bill said.

He highlighted the name of the AcceptPayment method. Doing so highlighted all the AcceptPayment methods that were written in the main file.

"And here it is again, and here it is again..." Bill said. "You see what I'm getting at?"

"Yeah," I said.

"Remember," Bill said, handing back my laptop, "Any time you write the same thing twice, you're probably not doing it the most efficient way."

"Do you think we should rewrite this stuff?" Arjun asked.

"No, I don't," Bill said. "You don't have the time for that. Just make it work."

We ended up rewriting the classes using inheritance, if for no other reason, so that Drew and Jack wouldn't make fun of us.

By lunch time of that second day of the capstone, we had all the classes rewritten and all the basics functioning. We had a fully stocked vending machine, which prompted the user to insert money, make a food selection, and then update the balance. Not bad, really.

Next, we had to address the dispensing of change. The challenge was that we had to tell exactly what type of denominations were coming back to the customers. We couldn't say, "Your change is $1.35," We had to say, "Your change is one dollar, one quarter, and one dime."

Arjun and I stared at the instructions that told us to do this and then we stared at our screens, thinking. Nothing was coming.

So I did what I always did when I couldn't think of a strategy. I just started typing. I knew that this was the same mistake we'd made the previous day. I knew that there must be some efficient, elegant way to do this correctly. But I also knew that this had to get done and time was running out. I typed and I typed and I typed.

Part of the assignment was that there must be eating sounds when the customer checked out, not actual audio that the app would make, but written onomatopoeia. So, if they bought one of the three bags of chips, our app should tell the customer something like, "Your change is one dime and one nickel. Crunch, crunch, crunch." Arjun worked on this aspect while I wrote the *War and Peace* of C# methods to provide the text for the change.

What I should have done was make a switch statement. A switch statement is a technique to use when you have many different "if" possibilities. Say you had to write logic for an app with many choices, like an app that someone could use to figure out how to cope with life during a boot camp. You could write, "If you get stuck, ask Bill and if you feel hungry, eat pretzels and if you become sad, drink three beers." But as the life adages start to pile up, the "`if`" statement will get out of control. This is when you need a switch. The switch for coping with a boot camp logic would look something like this:

```
Problem p = (Problem);

switch (p)
{
  case Problem.gotStuck:
    Console.WriteLine("Ask Bill.");
    break;

  case Problem.hungry:
    Console.WriteLine("Eat a fistful of pretzels");
    break;

  case Problem.sad:
    Console.WriteLine("Drink three beers");
    break;

  default:
    Console.WriteLine("Drink five beers");
    break;
}
```

It's a lot easier to read, it's a lot easier to write, and if you need to make changes to it, you just manipulate one or two lines of code. After nearly an hour of tinkering, it occurred to me that the change dispensing problem called for a switch statement. And I tried. I really did. But I couldn't get it to work. I don't know why. I'm sure it was some small syntactical mistake. I wrote it and received an error when I ran it. I rewrote and received a different error. I wrote it again and got a third, more detailed error. I then wrote the longest "`if`" statement that western civilization has ever seen.

It was approximately two hundred lines of code and took me all afternoon. But, by God, it worked.

While I was writing this obscenity, Arjun figured out the interface. It was getting near six o'clock on Friday evening, so it was time to face reality: we were going to have to come in on the weekend. When pondering the boot camp in December, I thought I might spend many weekends working. But the fact was, after five ten-to-twelve hour days in a row, working more on the weekend did not seem physically realistic. And, also, up until now, the workload hadn't yet demanded it.

Bill had cleared our schedule to work on the capstone, but regular class resumed on Monday, and we had to turn in the capstone by Tuesday morning. So, we decided to merge our work together and come in on Sunday to finish up.

To merge code meant that both Arjun and I would apply the code that we had on our local computers to the master source code. Remember the lessons about Git on day one? This process isn't difficult. Usually, there isn't a problem. Both your changes are applied to the master branch and all your work is saved congruously. But when you have two opposing changes written on the same line in the same file, this creates a merge conflict. You have told the code to do two different things in the same place and now you must decide which one you want to keep. If you've ever played a video game for hours and then realized you didn't save the game when you turned off the console, receiving a merge conflict message feels sort of like that. It's a demoralizing affair each and every time.

Arjun and I had some serious gaps in our knowledge. For instance, we did not know, somehow, that we should not be working in the same file at the same time. I'm not sure why we didn't realize this, I think the majority of the class had this basic understanding. Arjun and I chalked up our merge conflicts to bad luck. And, with this fatalistic attitude, they happened quite often.

Another gap in our knowledge was the ease with which these conflicts can be fixed if the two programmers simply put their heads together. The IDE makes it easy. An IDE is an integrated design environment. It's the software you use to write code, like how I'm using Google Docs to write this book. Our IDE was Microsoft's Visual Studio. And in Visual Studio, when you have a merge conflict it will ask you which change you want to keep. All you must do to resolve the conflict is choose one and move on. I think, for that first day, that Arjun and I just deleted the lines that conflicted and wrote them over. It was a mess and it kept us at the TE classrooms more than an hour later than we planned.

I arrived back at the House of Metal at ten o'clock on Sunday morning. Arjun was already there. Both of us felt refreshed and positive. All that remained was some cleanup and writing our daily sales to a file. That, and we had a little problem with the running total. Simple stuff. We should knock it out in two or three hours.

At five o'clock p.m., Arjun and I were sick of each other. Both of us wanted to quit. We had done our cleanup and we successfully wrote our sales to a CSV file for saving. But we couldn't figure out the problem with the goddamned balance. All of our code was in the main file, written and then written again in an inefficient clutter reminiscent of a back corner of a garage. If we had kept the method for the balance in one place, we'd be able to go to that file, debug it, and solve the problem. Instead, we had to troubleshoot the entire app over and over and over. We followed the balance like a mouse through a laboratory maze, beginning with $10.00. Then we buy a bag of chips for $3.50, and we have $6.50 left. Now we insert two more dollars and we have $8.50. Now we buy a pack of gum for $2.00, a bag of chips for $3.50, and a soda for $1.00. We check our balance...and it's zero dollars. Where the hell did it go? Start over. We feed $10.00 into our app...

This went on for some time.

We caught it eventually and I honestly can't even tell you what our problem was. When we found the reason why the balance was being set to zero, we fixed it, pushed our code to the master branch, closed our computers, and went home to drink.

Bill wasn't too hard on us during the demo of our vending machine. We had missed a couple of elements and our design was inarguably bad. But our app worked like a vending machine should work. Four weeks prior this would have been an impossible feat. And what neither Arjun nor I realized at the time was that we each learned quite a bit about version control and merging, the type of basic programming skills that will remain valuable throughout a career.

The other lesson the first capstone taught was that Daniel had been correct during his career path speech: I didn't want to work alone.

When the NPR ad for Tech Elevator first sparked my imagination, I didn't have a workplace in mind. At that juncture, my excitement was focused on the class and the adventure it portended. As the actual start date of the class approached, there may have been a fuzzy vision of where I would end up. It was a smaller company, I think, with a niche market in a hip part of town. I wasn't married to this idea, but it seemed like this was an ideal state.

After the first capstone, this image was shattered. I could see now what might happen if I was the only programmer at a company, or one of only a few. Problems would arise that I was not equipped to handle. I needed partners. And not only partners like Arjun to work side-by-side with, but more experienced people like Bill and Daniel to go to when a brick wall was hit. Yes, the small company grew smaller in my vision and tall office buildings loomed like beacons.

| Chapter Ten |

DIANE was the only woman in the .NET class. She was not the only woman in the program, but the other four (out of thirty-two students) were in the Java class. If that wasn't enough to make her isolated, she was the oldest person in the cohort as well. She is fit and dresses stylishly. She speaks well and is friendly in the right situations, though she seemed to distrust the idea that anyone in our class wanted to be friends with her. And she might have been right. I was the closest in age to Diane, but the majority of the .NET class were men in their twenties and early thirties. When the social conversations happened, they happened around Diane and not with her. Diane was never asked to play ping pong. When she was addressed, it was as if she were an aunt at a holiday dinner.

She was late for class every day. This stunned me at first. How could you pay this much for the boot camp and then miss the first fifteen minutes of every single class? It took until the second week before I realized that her lateness was due to childcare and that she had cleared her tardiness with the TE staff beforehand. It wasn't her fault, but this gave a rushed impression to her personality, always sneaking in while Bill was beginning his lecture and trying to quietly arrange her coat, her bag, her computer and its feet of cords.

Once she got settled in her seat, the quietness stopped. Diane asked more questions than the rest of the class combined. I don't want to seem like I'm against asking questions. I asked quite a few myself during Bill's lessons. And many times, some gray areas in the lesson that I was going to let remain gray were illuminated by Bill's answers to Diane's questions. But some of Diane's questions were not constructive for the whole class and should have been saved for one-on-one time with Bill. One might even say the questions were disruptive.

Diane's go-to move for question-asking was to raise her hand and at the same time say, "Soooooooo..." until Bill noticed and stopped speaking. When acknowledged in this manner, she would continue, "...you're saying that..." and then rephrase what Bill had just said. It was less of a question and more of a pause so that Diane could process the information at her own speed. Bill, writing on the whiteboard, would say, "When we write two plus signs after the variable 'i,' it becomes our iterator and will go up by one during each round of the for-loop." And Diane would say, "Soooooooo...you're saying that putting two plus signs after 'i' will make it increase by one during each round of the loop. And that's called an iterator."

"Yeah," Bill would answer.

Her other style of questioning was to ask what Bill was clearly about to tell us regardless of her question. There was an arch and a narrative to Bill's teaching, as if he was telling a joke with a punchline. Bill would say, "We created our variables for List A and List B outside the for-loop. List B is empty and List A has data. As we iterate through List A, we can add each item from List

A onto List B." This was when Diane's hand would raise, "So, how do we add to the list?" she would ask. "It's, uh, '.Add.' I was just about to tell you," Bill would say.

The questioning took up a lot of time and many of the queries were unnecessary. There was some eye-rolling from the class at large. Diane sat at the same table as Wayne, and with his constant muttering about "not getting it" and Diane's hand-raising addiction, the lectures could sometimes take on a jagged cadence.

I was paired with Diane for the lessons about SQL (pronounced "sequel"). SQL stands for Structured Query Language. It is the computer language used to communicate with databases. It's a declarative language, meaning that you're not trying to tell a computer what to do, but what you want from it. In C#, I had gotten used to telling the computer to loop through a list looking for certain variables with certain qualities and then to display them in the way of my choosing.

For example, in C#, if we tried to find cities in Pennsylvania with a population over a million, it would be two for-loops, probably, going through each list to find the information and a "`Console.WriteLine()`" to print it all out for us to see. Maybe ten lines of code. In SQL, it might look like this:

```
SELECT city FROM list WHERE population > 1000000
```

That's it. It's practically English.

To me, C# is a language that you must speak at a high level to do anything at all and SQL is like talking slowly and loudly because you think the computer can't hear you. It reminds me of going to Costa Rica and subjecting the Costa Ricans to my terrible Spanish. They can follow me as far as ordering a beer or asking where the bathroom is, but we're not going to launch a rocket to the moon with this level of communication. I'm sure SQL gets more complicated than the way I understand it, but the basics were more basic than C#.

Diane was a better programmer than I expected. A lot better, really. She was better than me. Because of her constant questions I thought she might struggle with the code, but she didn't. She had extensive notes that she referenced often and was able to solve several technical problems quickly that would have twisted my brain for half an hour.

And Diane is charming too. I am way closer in age to Diane than many of the other students and spending one-on-one time with her illuminated the things we had in common. Diane has children and she really likes to exercise. Those were the two big ones. But what I like most about Diane is that she dreams big and is utterly fearless while trying to make those dreams happen. I like to think that I share that quality, or, at least, I strive to.

Diane was one of the students who had hounded Daniel about working remotely during his career talk. Flexibility in the workplace was very important to her. Previous to Tech Elevator, she had worked some outside-sales jobs before starting her own fitness company in 2007. She did personal training, but she was also a master trainer, meaning she could teach a class to certify others to become personal trainers. When the business wasn't working out the way she had hoped after more than a decade, she turned to the boot camp. Diane felt a sense of urgency because of her age and she felt that the boot camp structure addressed this urgency.

The schedule that Diane had set up for herself was completely bonkers. I don't know if she underestimated the time commitment that Tech Elevator represented or if she just thought she'd have time to sleep in the summer, but she seemed pretty overbooked to me. Speaking to her well after all of this was over, she says she doesn't remember anyone from TE advising her to quit her job.

The children were her responsibility in the morning. Her husband went to work early, so she had to get them out of bed, spruced up for the day, and off to school. One was in preschool and one was in second grade. They attended school in two different buildings and the preschooler was only in for a half day. As I said before, she came to class late after dropping them off, rushing to settle into an eight to ten hour stint of learning to code. Her husband picked up the kids and met her at home where they would have dinner. Then, she went to bed.

No, she didn't. Just kidding.

Then, she went to the gym where she had clients whom she personally trained. This was in a four-hour-block from seven to eleven at night. She often fought to stay awake while working on the homework well-past midnight. She slept from two till six in the morning and then did it all over again.

And that's it. Pretty busy, right?

But that's *not* it. There's more.

Diane and I were in the middle of working on our database project. We had a fictional video rental store (Of *course* it was fictional; thanks, Netflix) where we had to create tables in a database representing the different genres of movies, the directors, the actors, the ratings, etc. It was fairly complicated, as we had only been studying databases for the last twenty-four hours, but Diane and I were making good progress.

After lunch she started getting phone calls. She left the room once, twice, three times. I figured it was something to do with her childcare. On occasion, Diane brought her son into Tech Elevator during the day. I don't know if he was sick during these days or if the school was closed for in-service, but he would sit in the main room and play on an iPad. During the breaks, Drew and Jack played Smash Brothers with him on the big monitors, letting him win most of the time.

The fourth phone call she took in the classroom rather than walking outside. I eavesdropped. I mean, I was sitting right next to her, working on the same project. I couldn't help but eavesdrop.

"I don't know," Diane said. "What unit sizes do they come in?"

She listened. She nodded her head.

"I guess I better go with two thousand then. How many rolls is that?"

I stopped pretending to type and started listening fully. *Is she buying two thousand rolls of toilet paper?*

"OK," she said. "And you still have my card on file? Yeah. Run it. Thanks."

Diane pressed "end" and set her phone on the desk. She looked at the computer screen.

"So, we're able to call a video by actor's last name, right?"

"What was that?" I asked, pointing at her phone.

"What? The call?"

"Yeah."

"I was buying stickers."

"You bought two thousand stickers?"

"Yeah."

"Why?"

She blushed and looked at the screen.

"I'm running for office."

"What? Like, a *political* office?"

"Yeah."

"What the hell, Diane? Where?"

"In McCandles. It's for town council."

"Shit..."

"I'm actually speaking tonight, so I wanted to have stickers to hand out."

"How do you have time to do this?"

She shrugged her shoulders and peered into the computer screen.

I have no idea how Diane managed all of these tasks. It was incredible. I felt like I had little time for anything besides the code. I helped out with Afton when I could, but Jenny took the lion's share of housework and childcare while I became lost in study. I could not have managed with even one more thing on my plate, I don't think. I certainly would have had to decline any nominations for political seats.

One thing that had been worrying me particularly was that I had not gone to any of the networking events that Caitie wanted us to attend. Each week on our chat board, Caitie posted different meet-ups and events for budding programmers and each week I found a reason not to go.

"We should hit one of these things," Craig said, frowning at the latest post from Caitie.

"I know..." I droned.

Jason slid his chair between us, looking at Craig's computer.

"You guys going to the Microsoft meetup?" he asked.

Jason sat right behind Craig and me at the next table and often liked to drift his office chair backwards between us with a quip or a question. He was a young, broad-shouldered kid of Scandinavian descent who had been a chef at a catering business before TE. He was big and imposing, but with a goofy smile and a rambunctious sense of humor. Though large and athletic, Jason was a straight computer nerd. He was also obsessed with World of Warcraft and Magic the Gathering. With enthusiasm for both video games and Magic, you might think he was fast friends with Craig, who shared these interests. Not really, though. They had diametrically opposite personalities. Where Craig was soft-spoken and thoughtful, Jason was impulsive and brash.

Jason had reached out to a former TE student before class had begun in January and the one recommendation he had latched onto was that the meet-ups and networking events should be well-attended. He went to all of them. Every meetup in every bar or office building that Caitie posted on the chat, Jason was there, shaking hands and giving elevator pitches. And each morning he would roll his chair between Craig and me to report what a great time it was and that he thought he may have forged some inroads at such and such a company.

Diane left early for one of her many activities, so I was done working on the pair programming for the day. Craig and Jason were two of the best students in the class, so they were often finished early. We decided to have a drink.

The meetup we planned to attend was sponsored by Microsoft. Pittsburgh's Microsoft offices are located in the Strip District, an area famous for its grocers, restaurants, and the availability of culturally diverse foods. This is the home of the Primanti's Sandwich.

This is the home of many of Pittsburgh's best breakfast diners. This is the place where you can get the best cuts of meat, the best selection of sushi-grade fish. And it also has a lot of bars.

We decided to head over to a bar called the Ten Penny before hitting the office building. We weren't sure what the meetup would be like. Many of the events had beer and food, but some were just about technology and social networking. If it was the latter kind, we each wanted to have a few drinks in the system to quell the nerves of meeting working software developers. We each threw down two beers and headed back out into the cold.

The office of Microsoft was the first place-of-work I had ever been that was clearly the domain of wealthy people. The turn-style front doors led to a spacious entryway with marble floors and friendly security guards, ready to usher you to the correct elevator for your meeting. Instead of pressing an "up" button for the elevator, you selected which floor you were off to, and one of six vessels came to pick you up. The inside of the elevator was discombobulating with its buttonlessness.

We got off on the fourteenth floor, to see a sleek, brown reception table, maybe twelve feet in length, with a digital screen behind it, the four squares of the Microsoft logo—green, blue, yellow, red—like the welcoming challenge of the Simon memory game. Everything was futuristic yet homey, the Starship Enterprise remodeled as a cruise ship. Cozy soundproof nooks were tucked in every corner, a kitchenette area had a stainless steel refrigerator, a Keurig, endless wrapped snack bars.

I was in awe. At Green Basil, I typed at a computer while flies landed on my face. At Barnes & Noble, I had to clean up puke on a shockingly regular basis. I had never worked in a place where I could use a bathroom that wasn't open to the public. The Microsoft offices brought a tear to my eye.

The conference room we entered housed a series of desks that sat two people each. The chairs were soft and comfortable and the desks were tricked out with enough outlets to power a mansion at Christmastime. Where walls should have been were floor-to-ceiling windows displaying the Monongahela River, the Fort Pitt Bridge, the Inclines of Pittsburgh inching to the crest of Mt. Washington.

And there was pizza!

The room was already crowded, so we didn't have our choice of seats. Craig, Jason and I each took a slice of pizza before sitting. Craig and I managed to find an open desk for the two of us, but Jason sat next to a stranger. He immediately shook the man's hand. "Hi, I'm Jason and I'm a student at Tech Elevator. I've always been interested in computers, but my first passion was for food. . . "

And so on.

The meeting was late getting started, so Craig and I ate pizza and chatted. A funny thing about mine and Craig's relationship—we had become good friends without ever drinking together. Almost every friendship I've made from college and beyond was made over drinks. Craig and I had shared stories about our families, about our childhoods and significant others, we had laughed to tears on several occasions, all without the warm, fuzzy aid of a few beers.

Now that we had this aid, things got serious in a hurry.

"We should hang out," I said, definitively. "I mean, I know we see each other all day every day, but we should hang out too."

"Oh, yeah," Craig said, throwing up his hands as if I had read his mind, "I mean, we're gonna be friends, like, for *forever*."

"Yes," I agreed.

"You're cool," Craig told me.

"So are you," I replied.

And this was after only two beers. Two beers drunk at precisely the right time can change the world. I really believe that.

A young man with the literary name of John VanSickle took center stage and thanked everyone for coming. There were nearly forty people in the room, way more than I expected. He talked about how he wanted to do more of these meetups and how Microsoft had offered the space on a weekly basis. He then started his presentation about some software called SignalR. SignalR had something to do with Asp.NET, which we were just beginning to learn about at TE and a way to use Asp.NET and SignalR for mobile phone messaging. I did not understand even a little bit of what John VanSickle said.

After the presentation Jason, Craig, and I hung around and had a series of awkward conversations with other programmers, many who were also job-seeking. When anyone heard that we were in a boot camp, they asked a few polite questions and moved along, looking for someone with a little more hiring power.

I said goodnight and walked out into the brisk night air to find my car. I drove home listening to an old REM album. I thought about my new friendship with Craig and felt bad that Diane, because of biases of age and gender, was kept out of new friendships from the program. I poured a glass of whiskey when I got home and sat down to watch Survivor with my wife and daughter while Diane was leaving her political rally to go work a four-hour shift at the gym. I had been sound asleep for hours by the time Diane left work, hustling in the cold to get back home so she could do her schoolwork. Diane's life was as complicated and as packed with info as C#, and I felt lucky to maintain a SQL-kind-of-existence for as long as I could.

| Chapter Eleven |

JACK was only nineteen years old when he showed up for the first day of Tech Elevator. He had gone to college, bent on the traditional path of a computer science degree, and then dropped out after one semester. He's tall and thin with brown, spiky hair, like an Anime character. He has round features, blue eyes, and no ability to grow facial hair. Commenting on this last feature, he once rubbed his chin and sang "Smooth boy for life!"

When Jack is happy with something, say, at the success of a certain line of code or because people have agreed to go to Taco Bell with him, he makes a specific movement with his right arm that under different circumstances might be described as a tic. I only don't describe the movement as a tic because he seemingly does it on purpose and not as part of a compulsion and because he encourages others to do it with him. It goes like this: he flips his arm out and spreads his fingers as if he is a waiter carrying a tray. Then, after a jaunty pause, he flips the mimed tray over, often accompanying the movement with a "Boom!" or an "Aw, yeah!"

I don't know why he does this, but it makes me laugh. It makes everyone laugh. He got Bill to do it once and the class basically exploded.

Jack is from Cincinnati, Ohio, and his parents, both programmers, still live there. He dropped out of college for several reasons, the top two being that he did not like the social environment and he thought the classes moved too slowly. Also, he's interested in investing and the way money works. When it became clear to him that he could spend 80 percent less money and three and a half years less time and still have the same result—a job as a developer—he quit school and rented an apartment in Pittsburgh. He started the boot camp life.

Coding boot camps aren't for everyone, but neither are four-year computer science degrees. Will a student coming out of a four-year program know more than a coding boot camp graduate? Yes. Almost certainly. Will they land a better job? Maybe, maybe not. In 2019, computer science majors were earning an average of $68,000 a year at their first job. That's ten grand higher than what Tech Elevator was promising. However, the average computer science degree costs more than $100,000 dollars. They may have more refined skills which could lead to quicker and larger raises. But they will also have about ten more years of debt. Some younger people have started making the choice of less debt.

Drew was another one of these younger people. Also nineteen years old, Drew has black messy hair, thick glasses, and an irreverent tone in everything he says. He had almost the same story as Jack—he went to college for a couple of months, thought it was too slow and too wasteful and dropped out for the boot camp.

Drew was obviously a good and somewhat experienced coder before he ever came to Tech Elevator. He had built websites and knew enough JavaScript to be dangerous. He had tried to get a job as a programmer straight out of high school without a degree, but no one would interview him. He seemed overly confident but would occasionally confess to anxieties that stood in opposition to most of his behavior. He was something of a smart aleck and, though he clearly tried to be kind to people he met, inferior coders knew they were inferior around him. He had some habits that weren't great for the classroom and these habits probably contributed to him dropping out of college even though he touted the move as pure common sense. Only one of these habits irked Bill. Drew had a problem with falling asleep in class.

I noticed during the third week, right before the capstone, that Drew had nodded off during Bill's lecture. When I pointed it out to Craig, he half-frowned and shook his head.

"Yeah. He's been doing that almost every class. Fancy has a really good picture of it, actually."

The picture was ludicrous. It had been taken two days before while we were learning about Lists and Dictionaries. The picture on Fancy's phone shows Drew's laptop pushed to the side and Drew's forehead flat on the white surface of the desk, his arms dangling at his side. He looked like a mob hit.

And like Rick Fancy, Bill had christened Jack and Drew with nicknames that stuck. During our database study, the Socrative quizzes contained an odd name that kept surfacing: Jack Heartless. The other names used in the quiz questions were more traditional—Brian Harmon, Christopher Miller, Amber Tipton. But again and again during the quizzes, Jack Heartless would be used in an SQL question. The data was always listed with the last name first so that it read Heartless, Jack. When the name read aloud got a couple laughs, Bill started nodding his head, like he does when he knows he's got his audience on the hook.

"Sounds like a pirate, doesn't it? Heartless Jack."

Students turned to look at Jack, who was turning slightly red.

"Yeah, Heartless Jack," Bill continued, savoring the line he had saved up, "and his sidekick Sleeping Drew!"

The use of the nickname Sleeping Drew was inconsistent, usually only occurring when Drew was actually sleeping in class. But Heartless Jack had legs.

In no way is Jack cold or cruel and I think this might be why the name seemed so right. Jack's sense of humor, like many smart, young people, tended toward the absurd. Having a nickname that in no way fit him somehow fit him perfectly. And I don't think Jack minded being Heartless. He would occasionally do the hand thing when someone called him by the moniker.

That week, I was the luckiest person in class because I drew Jack as my partner for the second capstone. When I saw our names written next to each other, I turned and looked back to where Jack sat, next to Drew in the back of the class. He smiled and nodded at me. He did the hand thing.

The second capstone was called National Parks. It was, like the Vending Machine capstone, a command-line application. There would once again be no visual front end; it would be completely text-based. The main thrust of the assignment was to make a reservation system that served five national parks. The user should be able to choose a park from a menu, read a bit about it, see the different campsites available, and make a reservation to stay there. The names of the parks and a short, descriptive paragraph about them were given to us as our data. The challenge of this capstone was all about the databases. We were given the database with the info on the parks within, but we had to access it through code, display the information in a sensible way on the screen, and then write reservations to the database.

"This is going to be fun," I said.

"Oh, yeah," Jack agreed. "I'm totally stoked for this. I just want to treat it like a *job*, you know? Like we have our work and we have to turn it in *exactly* right."

"Yes," I said.

Jack's enthusiasm for the project was bubbling over. As the morning progressed we moved past the staging phase and started, in quick fashion, to code. It became clear that the challenges of this capstone were going to be different than the challenges I had faced in other pair programming situations. Before, when partnered up, I sometimes had to carry the team. And even when I didn't have to carry the team, I was always the one with an eye on the clock making sure that we didn't waste our time on a small detail, which would result in unfinished work. But instead of carrying the team, my main challenge was going to be keeping up with Jack and making sure I was useful.

Jack's effortlessness is what surprised me most. The things we had drilled—making classes, switch statements, for-loops, I could at this point bust out from memory alone. Jack did almost *everything* from memory. Long complicated procedures, some of which I had forgotten or never heard of, sprang from his fingers like he was copying down a nursery rhyme. And when we didn't know something, Jack's Googling skills were unparallelled. Of course I was studied in the art of finding answers to questions on Stackoverflow (a question-and-answer forum that literally every programmer in the world uses), but the problem came when I had to apply what I found to my code. I could never get the code on Stackoverflow to work like it was supposed to. Jack did not have this problem. The solutions on Stackoverflow blended like milk in coffee with his code.

Jack was nineteen and I was thirty-nine. Had I had a child when I was twenty, he would have been Jack's age. Once, without thinking, I said to Jack, "You would have hated me when I was your age." I said this on a whim, but later on that day it opened up a rabbit hole of memories, a hallway of mirrors and possibilities.

Since the conception of my Tech Elevator adventure, this thought had lurked: what if I would have done something like this boot camp instead of going to college?

For many reasons, this is a pointless question. For starters, there were no computer boot camps in 1998 when I graduated from high school.

So, suppose I went to college for computer science rather than English? One could argue that I would have gotten a higher paying job out of college, learned skills that were extremely rare in the workforce at the time, maybe even have hitched my star to one of the companies in the dot com rise and become a millionaire, if not by skill, then by being in the right place at the right time.

I have no regrets like that. None at all. Mainly because it wouldn't have happened.

I was a really good kid when I was little. I was polite to adults, got good grades, and didn't get into fights with anyone but my sister. I remained polite and compromising throughout school and still am today. But right around the age of thirteen, I developed two interests that never went away. The first was a fascination with girls. And, really, this wasn't new at thirteen. I had been interested in the opposite sex as far back as I can remember. Some people don't care about these matters until puberty, but I had been secretly stealing kisses since kindergarten. At the age of thirteen it became socially acceptable for me to be dating, so that's what I did. A lot.

The other habit that sort of came out of nowhere was the use of drugs and alcohol. So often you hear these stories about addiction coupled with horrible parents or abusive experiences. I had nothing of the sort. My parents are lovely people and did a fantastic job providing a safe and nurturing environment for me—so much so that I named my child Afton, after the street where I grew up. I did this as a sort of blessing that she would have as good a childhood as I did.

But still.

I have always been interested in the way that drugs affect my mind. Even something as silly as taking an extra Tylenol PM or doubling my dose of NyQuil when I have a cold feels like an exciting science experiment to me. Beer was hilarious. Marijuana scary, but still intriguing. Sure, I had other hobbies. I was into skateboarding, I played saxophone and guitar, I became obsessed with reading after discovering the *Dragonlance Chronicles*, and I've always been a writer. But I would drop any of these pastimes if Adeep called to report that he got his fifteen-year-old hands on a bottle of whiskey. And so the next few years became a never-ending quest to acquire some type of intoxicant and then hang out with girls.

As you can imagine, this came with its fair share of trouble. I was brought home by the police twice for alcohol, and I was caught by other authorities on several different occasions. There was time spent grounded, some anger from my parents, some friends I wasn't allowed to see for a while. There were serious talks about addiction and even a therapist brought in at one point. I have terrible genes as far as addiction goes, both of my grandfathers having been full-blown alcoholics. On my dad's side, my grandfather Ted was a beloved figure. He was a fireman and a drinker, and he was loud and funny. People thought he was a riot and he died in 1984 from the hole he drank into his liver. It was a little different on my mother's side. I don't believe I've ever seen a picture of that grandfather.

With that background, it's no surprise that my parents were concerned. Whereas some of their contemporaries would turn a blind eye to the drinking when their children turned seventeen and eighteen, my parents did not. In their view, it was illegal because I was not twenty-one. This was a logical argument and true, but I would, upon being caught once again, complain about it.

They were justified, don't get me wrong. I was not responsible and needed as many roadblocks as could be set up to stop me from hurting myself. Early on, I would get home from school, pour myself three fingers of neat whiskey (all of the liquor in my parents' cabinet was water by the time I was fifteen), and watch my after-school cartoons. When in high school, I stayed out until my curfew, came home, and then sneaked out the side door to go back to the party. The lowest of the low was the morning my dad found vomit down the side of the driver's side door of the car. I had apparently thrown up out of the window, possibly while driving. I don't remember.

My dad cried that day when confronting me about the drunk driving. He didn't yell because he could hardly speak for the tears. He knew what I finally know now, looking back: that just by fate had I not killed someone or myself. That my carelessness was legitimately dangerous, like a tiger kept as a pet. That I had to consider the feelings of others in my actions and become a better person. I took all he had to say and said nothing in return. I didn't even apologize. My teenage hormones and stubborn attitude spun a web of sociopathy around my emotions. This is what I knew: I could not be hurt, but I could hurt others.

There is a feeling of invincibility that comes with thoughts like that, and I lived like these feelings were as true as gravity. I was horribly invincible.

It took me a long time to grow out of that attitude, to be able to feel bad when I do something selfish. But I did. I have. I feel terrible about drunk driving, the worry I put my parents through, and plenty of other jangled moments. But feeling bad is one thing, not repeating the action another.

The drugs and alcohol affected my grades, too, though it's taken me twenty years to admit that. I normally received As or Bs without much work, but once, in the seventh grade, I got a D. In English of all things. English! I just hadn't done the work. I had spaced out, didn't listen to my teacher, didn't do the reading. My mother was furious.

The only other time I scored truly bad grades was freshman year of college. The first semester I came back with a 1.7 grade point average. I had taken another D, this time in a Psych 101 class for which I didn't even bother to buy the textbook. What would Freud have to say about that? My parents threatened to take me out of college after these grades got back to them. And that was one thing I could not abide.

College was a little utopia for me, and I think the fear of leaving that environment where everyone had the same interests (intoxicants and our budding sexualities) kickstarted my will to learn. Or maybe it was my will to survive.

Either way, I battled back. I started actually studying for the first time in my life and I didn't miss a class from sophomore year until I graduated. I remember reading *A Midsummer Night's Dream* in a Shakespeare class. While a student in high school, I read the assigned work and usually understood it on a pretty deep level the first time through. But if I didn't, because it was written in antiquated language or because I found it dull, I would just skim or skip large parts and roll the dice on the test. In college, after I scored a C on my *Love's Labour's Lost* test, I knew I could not afford to do that with this Shakespeare class. If I didn't understand a section of *Midsummer Night's Dream*, I read it again. If I didn't know a word, I looked it up. And wouldn't you know it, I started to understand. I even started to enjoy it. Shocker: Shakespeare is really good.

I received mostly As for the remainder of college. I graduated in four years, and though I was academically sound for three of them, my grade point average could never really recover from that first semester. I left college with a 2.9. It didn't bug me at the time. I was working within a month of graduation and no one was asking about my GPA. But at one point, when unhappy with my place at Barnes & Noble, I applied to the University of Pittsburgh for their master's program in writing. They wouldn't even talk to me unless I had a 3.0. Ten years had passed since that D in Psych. I felt pretty hollow about that one.

The year I got that D, I was the same age as Jack during Tech Elevator. Here he was, working with an adult (I mean me, when I say "adult") and doing the lion's share of the work, picking up the bulk of the responsibility. And he was thrilled to be doing it. So, when I wonder if it was a fault in planning when I chose an English degree over learning to program at the age of nineteen, the answer is easy: no. Absolutely not.

The programming wasn't an option. Not only would nineteen-year-old Sean have scoffed at the idea, he wasn't equipped to follow through. I don't believe I would have made it through the first week at Tech Elevator had I arrived in 1999. I would have been hung over, clueless, and scared. I would have flirted with the one younger girl in the Java class and I probably would have been asked to leave halfway through the program.

Jack would have hated me. As well he should.

In Joan Didion's memoir, *The Year of Magical Thinking*, she quotes Delmore Schwartz, writing "Time is the school in which we learn." I concur. Maturity over time was why I could attend Tech Elevator at thirty-nine but would not have stood a chance at nineteen. But there was something else too. The reason I had to have an English degree and not one in computers or business. I don't know that I've ever said this out loud or told anyone, but I consider myself an artist.

What do I mean by this? Am I talking about being a writer? Well, yes. I am. But the music I play. And when I draw. Even sometimes when I'm listening to music or reading someone else's writing, whenever I feel deeply, I am testifying to the fact that I am an artist. It embarasses me to admit this, mainly because I do not make a living by selling my art. But at my core, I am someone who appreciates and creates art. This is the first foundation of my soul, the binary in which my being is written, lower down than anything else.

This foundation has its good attributes along with its bad. In my twenties, the period in which I started to seriously practice writing, my art gave me the power for true introspection. I wrote and I read and I saw myself for maybe the first time. I didn't love what I saw there. I was a drunk, for the most part. I didn't work very hard. I didn't have the respect for women that I should have. I didn't value my friendships or my family in any serious way. I was walled off emotionally. I was so fortunate to be surrounded by people who wanted to be my friend, my family, my lover, and I still felt lonely most of the time.

I used my art as a mirror. I tore down the image I saw and rebuilt myself as someone who is trustworthy and hardworking and loving. I think the regular routine of receiving rejections from literary agents and publishing houses helped a lot. When a hurtful rejection came, I felt bad for a day. But in the days and weeks following, I taught myself to get back up. This is when I learned to never,

never feel bad for myself. I became invincible again, not through cold indifference but through striving toward self-improvement.

This is a good thing that art has given me.

But, if I am to talk about my engine for self-improvement, I must also talk about the fuel—delusion.

When we're young in America, we always think we're going to be famous. Children believe they will be a basketball player, the president of the United States, an astronaut. But as we get older, we bring these goals back down to earth—lawyer, teacher, nurse. Just the other day, my fourteen-year-old nephew told me he wanted to be a sports therapist. I found the rationality of his dreams shocking.

Because this is not the case with those who fancy themselves artists. Or, maybe I shouldn't speak for all of us. It's not the case for me. When I was in high school, I was completely sure that I would be both a known writer and a singer in a band. When I was in college I knew that most of my friends and I would soon comprise a movement that would change the landscape of poetry. And after college, all through my twenties, every cold morning I had to slouch toward the Forest Hills Barnes & Noble at five in the morning, I repeated a mantra that it was only a matter of time before I finished the novel I was working on and everything changed.

I'm not cured of this, by the way. Just because I can confess my vanity and point at my delusion does not mean that I don't still swoon for it. If my body is a temple, then it is a temple haunted by three ghosts, the names of which are vanity, addiction, and hedonism. None of what I've been discussing in this chapter is completely in the past. I've pushed those ghosts to the basement, but now and then I walk down the creaky stairs to play cards with them. I'm drinking a beer as I write this.

I don't drink as much now because I don't like to be sick. Those hangovers get worse as you approach forty. And I suppose my expectations for fame have been tempered some too. I might hope for just a publication now rather than the riches. I might look upon my manuscripts as lottery tickets that I turn in every few years to literary agents, waiting for one to hit big. But I still think one is going to hit. Hell, I think *this* one might hit.

Any day now. Any day now, you'll see how smart I am.

I know that Jack would have hated the nineteen-year-old Sean, but I think he likes the thirty-nine-year-old version. We don't have a ton in common. He lives by himself in an apartment, plays video games, hangs out with friends, and loves, *loves* computers. I live with a wife and daughter and spend most of my free time making up stories. But we both work hard, we both appreciate the other's skills, and, damn it, we're both polite and compromising.

I didn't shake Jack's hand as we walked out of the stellar review of our capstone that Bill had just given us. It would have been weird to shake his hand. But I smiled and slapped the side of my computer.

"That was great!"

"Yeah!" he agreed.

"Hey, thanks for all your work on this," I said. "You did a really fantastic job. And I know that if I had another partner this would have been way tougher."

"No prob," he said. "You did awesome too."

He did the hand thing.

"Aw yeah!"

I did the hand thing.

"Boom!"

| Chapter Twelve |

AFTER the second capstone, things started moving at an alarming rate. So far, our entire education was concerned with what the industry calls the "back end." The back end focuses on the methods and algorithms that make things function and the databases where the information is kept. You will recall that both capstones, the vending machine and the national parks database were command line applications. There were no visuals save the text instructions leading the user through the page. Finally, after seven weeks of class, we were delving into the front end. Finally, our finished products would look like websites.

In the months leading up to Tech Elevator I studied HTML, CSS, and JavaScript. From this study, I found HTML and CSS simpler than JavaScript, but JavaScript more enjoyable. JavaScript is back-endy, you write functions with it and it makes your website do stuff—a word changes color as you hover over it, two numbers inputted are added together, the temperature is translated from Celsius to Fahrenheit. HTML is all about layout and CSS (Cascading Style Sheets) is concerned with styling that layout with fonts, colors, and outlines. When I saw HTML and CSS on the menu for week eight, I'll admit I was relieved. I was ready for something easy.

Why hadn't I learned yet that nothing was going to be easy? I honestly can't say.

Bill went through the tags and layouts of the styling languages. Some of it I recognized from my study and much of it I did not. The things one could do with these languages was many times more complicated than I had previously conceived. Whereas I had simply added tags to create a basic structure for a website, there was an entire child/parent relationship to them that I had only glossed over in my pre-study. My head swam with the labyrinthine intricacies.

The front end lessons had a different vibe than the back end lessons. Bill read his notes in silence for long stretches of time before speaking. The examples didn't have much life to them, his answers to questions were brief, very un-Bill-like.

And the homework was different too. Instead of a series of exercises, we were just given two documents—one styled with CSS and the other with an identical HTML structure but no CSS. Our assignment? Make one look like the other.

There are many differences between back end development and front end development, but in my opinion the most important distinction is error messages. When using Visual Studio as your IDE and working with C#, if you do something wrong, a red squiggly line appears under your bunk line of code, like when you mispell a word when typing in Google Docs. You can then hover over that line of code, and the IDE will give you suggestions on what you might want instead. In fact, when you write code in Visual Studio, it is, like an over-excited concierge, constantly suggesting what you might want to write next. If you were to write `word.Substring(2,5)`, a quick little string-slicer that would return part of a word instead of the whole thing, Visual Studio would be by your side the whole way, politely offering up recommendations. When you write "`word`" and ".", a drop-down appears with scores of choices from the .NET framework about what you might want to type next. In fact, you don't even have to type it. You might just write "S" and press enter for the word "`Substring`" to appear. Visual Studio practically writes the code for you.

This is not the way with CSS. With CSS, you make a slew of changes, save your work, and then check the document to see if your changes are what you expect. It can be frustrating as a beginner because more often than not, nothing has changed. It has to do with that parent/child relationship between the HTML tags. The trick is to make sure you are calling out the correct element on the page, to follow the path of tags until you reach your intended target. But the trickier trick is, if you're not doing it correctly, CSS isn't going to tell you why. There are no error messages, no way to debug, nothing to do but try and try again.

The website we were tasked with recreating was the homepage for a pumpkin patch with large orange pumpkins and promises of hayrides. The sixteen of us in the .NET class sat at our desks making small changes to the style sheet, saving the work, and then twisting our faces in confusion as we looked back at the website to see either no evidence of the changes we had just made or, worse, the pumpkins stretched into ungodly shapes across the screen, like a Dali representation of a cider festival.

Craig and I, working on our individual projects, toiled in silence but for the occasional "What the fucks" when ten minutes of work yielded no progress. After an hour and a half of wading in CSS quicksand, we noticed Wayne in the Elevate Space, holding his racket and bouncing a ping pong ball on the table.

"Is Wayne just not doing this assignment?" I posed to Craig.

Before Craig could answer, Jason rolled his chair between us, his large, blond head blocking Craig's face from my vision.

"He's done," Jason said.

"What?"

"Wayne," Jason said, raising his eyebrows. "He's fucking done. He finished already."

It was almost impossible to believe. Wayne, who spent the first seven weeks reporting to anyone who would listen that he did not get this stuff, had finished his front end homework before everyone except for Drew and Jack (who always finished first).

"How is that possible?" Craig asked, looking skeptically through the glass door to where Wayne was now bouncing the ping pong ball repeatedly toward the ceiling.

"I don't know," Jason said, sliding back to his computer. "Motherfucker just gets it."

And that's what it is with CSS—some people get it and some people don't. Wayne? That motherfucker *got it.* It's like decorating a living room or dressing yourself properly—some people can do it well without thinking too much and others wear shorts and sandals with a sweater.

This goes to all levels of programmers. One of the biggest problems with our front end assignments was that we couldn't really go to Bill with questions. Because he didn't have the answers.

"I don't know," Bill said, stroking his gray ponytail as it hung over his shoulder like a pet. "This is the stuff I hire other people to do."

Bill is a back end guy, through and through.

"Just keep fiddling with it till it looks right."

The idea that practice makes perfect seemed to be the central strategy in the Tech Elevator curriculum for dealing with front end programming. We had to be good at front end work, so we did a lot of it. The homework, which had seemed excessive before, now came in colossal, unthinkable waves.

After two days of HTML and CSS homework, we were introduced to a website architecture strategy called MVC. MVC stands for Model/View/Controller. This was the Rosetta Stone of our education, in many ways. Everything that we had learned so far was tied together in the MVC lessons.

It's like this: The Model in MVC is the data. You have variables that your website deals with listed here and a file called the DAL (Data Access Layer) that retrieves data from a database. The View part of MVC is the front end. This part is concerned with how the data is displayed for the user. The Controller part Bill likened to a traffic cop. This is the go-between for the front and back ends, telling the data to go here or go there. The Controller is the key to functionality. This is the first time it occurred to me that programming, and truly the entire Internet, is only about one thing—moving and displaying data.

And we were going to move a lot. I wasn't finished with the second day of CSS homework when the MVC stuff started getting piled on top. Each day we had another lesson about how MVC works and each day Bill would assign both group and individual homework. I thought I was lucky because I was paired with Fancy and Jason, both who were better than me and faster than me at most things programming. But it didn't really matter—the front end work had made novices of us all. Our trio struggled mightily taking a dozen steps forward to find we were still in the same place. We worked all afternoon and it seemed like we had accomplished about ten minutes of work. It was discouraging. And I still had the individual assignments to contend with.

Some time around the database work with Diane, I had decided that I wouldn't kill myself over getting threes on the homework anymore. For the first few weeks of the cohort, if I couldn't finish an assignment I pestered other students to get the answers and then studied what they had done after turning it in. Everyone did this, there was a commune feel to the work, to some degree. We had to have those threes on the homework. It was stated in our Tech Elevator contract that TE had the right to ask us to leave if at any time we were averaging less than a one. Now, seven weeks in, I could probably skip homework for the rest of the program before my average sunk that low. So when I looked up on Thursday of that week and realized that I hadn't finished even one assignment completely, I started to work a new strategy: turn the shit in, done or not.

This might sound like I was slacking off, and maybe I was just a little, but if you put in ten-to-twelve-hour days of utter concentration five days in a row, there isn't much more that can be done. I turned in all of that week's homework more or less on time. I received three twos and two ones. I felt bad when I saw the scores but I also felt as though I couldn't have possibly worked any harder. My brain was turning to mush and I walked around in a daze when I wasn't focusing on the TE assignments.

The thing is, the assignments weren't just about coding. There was Pathway work in there too. We had drafts of our résumés due to Caitie every week. We had workshops to attend that taught us different interview techniques, and, of course, the workshops had homework of their own. And several times a week, TE brought in different companies to speak to us—FedEx, FBK Banking, BNY Mellon. The companies bought us lunch and then pitched what it would be like to work for them.

The lunches were both good and bad. We ate first, which was nice. But then, fat and comfortable, we had to stand, one at a time in front of our chairs, and deliver our elevator pitches. After listening to our wooden blurbs, the speaker took us through a day-in-the-life of a programmer who worked for their company. They fielded some questions afterward and then it was time for networking. Some of the reps seemed like they were selling to us and some of them seemed like we had to sell ourselves to them. But either way, there was an awkward crowding around the person or persons from the company. TE students, myself included, lingered with painful smiles asking canned questions, trying our best to network and make Caitie proud.

While these lunches were incredibly valuable for the information we received and the connections we could possibly make, they hurt our schoolwork in a few different ways. The first was simply the time that was sucked up by them. Normally, lunch was eaten in ten or fifteen minutes and then back to coding. Sometimes a ping pong game was played. The company lunches took two solid hours when the eating, presentation, and networking was considered. In a week of double homework, this just didn't fly.

The other problem was that we had to be "on" during the company lunches. Even if we only took fifteen minutes for lunch, it was fifteen minutes of *our* time. You could talk to a friend, watch something on your phone, stare at the goddamned wall, whatever. The company lunches robbed you of this downtime and kept the stress ball rolling.

And the stress was real. As students at Tech Elevator, we feared many things, but there was something that scared us more than the homework, more than delivering elevator pitches, and more than turning our résumés in on time. That something was the date March 18.

March 18 was the day that Caitie had listed as the earliest that we were allowed to apply to jobs. The date had seemed delightfully nestled in the distant future for all of the cohort, but now we raised our heads from our warrens of coding homework to see that it was the first day of March and the dreaded deadline was just around the corner.

You see, all of the lessons that we were learning, from the programming to the social networking, were studied in a theoretical vacuum. The vacuum made us forget the stakes; it made learning easy(ish) and fun. But in reality, we weren't at computer camp. We *had* to make this thing work out. There was a lot of money on the table. And the only mark of success was whether or not you got the job at the end of the program.

So I had to take it seriously when Caitie set up mock interviews. We were to sit with Caitie as she conducted a behavioral interview with us and then immediately critiqued our performance. I felt woefully unprepared for such a task. And it killed me that I had to cut time away from CSS and MVC to practice some non-acronym skills (NAS?) like answering behavioral interview questions.

I am not an experienced interviewer. For my first job? The terrible one as the copywriter in Secaucus? My friend Tim told his boss about me and then I was asked to drive out to New Jersey and start working. No interview. I interviewed for Barnes & Noble after that, but you basically got hired at B&N if you could read and didn't smell like pot during the interview. I know. I conducted many interviews on behalf of Barnes & Noble and turned away scores of applicants who could not fit this criteria. I applied for a few other jobs over the course of my B&N tenure, but I didn't get any offers. When the time came to find a job as a software developer, I would be thirty-nine years old and walking into maybe my fifth or sixth real interview ever. This made me quite uneasy.

So what do I do when I feel uneasy about something? I formulate a plan. I over-prepare. Caitie had shared a document of behavioral questions that she asked us to read before the mock interviews. *Tell me about a time when you had to work with someone whose personality was very different from yours. Tell me about a time when you had to learn something quickly to perform your job. Tell me about a time when you made a mistake. Tell me about a time...*

I contemplated these questions, and while I did so I kept a notepad on which to write down stories as I went. There were twenty-some questions that Caitie had given us and I chronicled seven or eight work tales that I thought I could pigeon-hole into any of the queries. I memorized these stories. No, not word-for-word, but the general gist of them. The idea is that I had them in my pocket when the questions came and I could twist them, bend the plots and the facts, to answer anything that might be thrown my way.

The mock interview was stranger than I thought. Since Caitie was conducting all the interviews herself, we were taking them in groups. I was in with three other people: Drew, one of the nineteen-year-old-wiz-kids, Christopher, he-who-did-not-want-to-work-at-Reynolds Sportswear, and April, a young woman from the Java class—brown hair with sharp bangs, sarcastic in a likeable, witty sort of way. The extra strangeness came not only in us being in the room as others answered Caitie's questions, but we were also supposed to pose as interviewers ourselves. We were supposed to supply critiques to our classmates.

April went first and she did pretty well. She had worked at a psychiatric ward before attending Tech Elevator. Her stories therefore were always concerned with nursing and the mentally ill. Her answers centered on empathy and duty and I thought she came off well, if maybe a little too quiet in her delivery.

Christopher started off well, too, but it was clear that he was very nervous. If you recall, Christopher was so nervous about the first delivery of the elevator pitches that he spoke with Caitie privately about going first so that he could get it out of the way. I didn't see his nerves surface during that elevator pitch, but they did here in the mock interview. He leaned forward to answer Caitie's question, his intense eyes locking with hers. He spoke about living in Russia as a student and the difficulties thereof. Caitie nodded at one point, in recognition of something Christopher had said. Christopher stopped speaking.

"What. . . ?"

"Oh. Nothing," Caitie said, suddenly flustered.

"I thought you wanted to say something," Christopher said, narrowing his eyes. "You were nodding?"

"I was just acknowledging what you were saying," Caitie told him. "Go ahead."

"OK," Christopher said, looking down at the table.

There was a few seconds of silence.

"I can't continue. Just move on," Christopher told her. "I'll get the next one."

Drew was up next. He peered at Caitie through his blocky glasses, a tuft of his thick black hair pointing at the ceiling, the rest smashed to the left. He kept something of his normal sardonic expression on his face, but his hands tightly gripped a pen in front of him, twisting and turning.

"OK. . . " Caitie said, looking through her sheet of behavioral questions. "Tell me about a time when your team or company was undergoing a change. How did that change affect you and how did you react?"

"Ummmm. . ."

Some moments of silence.

"You can take your time," Caitie told him. "Your interviewer will not think less of you if you sit for a while in silence and think of your answer."

Caitie gave this piece of advice a lot. I'm not sure I agree with her. No one likes silence.

"Yeah, all right," Drew said. Then after a pause, "Could you say the question again?"

Caitie repeated the question.

"I mean, I don't know," Drew said. And then he didn't say anything else.

"OK," Caitie said, nodding her head. "Well, let's think of a time at work where something was changing. Has that ever happened at a place where you worked?"

Drew smiled in a small way. "I mean, should I really talk about working at Target?"

"Sure!" Caitie said. "Of course, you should."

"Yeah. I just don't think these people are going to care about me working a cash register at Target."

He has a point, I thought. I worried about the same thing. Who in the tech industry was going to want to hear my stories about working in retail? One had absolutely nothing to do with the other. I had tried to gear my answers toward management skills and problem-solving, but what would I say if I had only worked at a cash register like Drew?

"No!" Caitie insisted. "You're wrong, Drew. Your experience *does* matter."

"OK," Drew said. He thought for a while. "I guess, once, at Target, the registers were updated and all of the buttons you were supposed to push were in a different place. It confused people. I helped out with that."

"OK, good," Caitie said. "And how were you able to help out?"

"Well, I could still use the registers," he said. "I didn't think they were that much different, but everyone else was really confused. So I showed them where all the new stuff was."

"Great!" Caitie said. "And what lesson did you learn from this experience?"

"Huh?"

"Remember, you want to address the questions, tell how you were challenged, how you overcame that challenge, and what you learned from it. So, what did you learn from this experience?"

"I. . . learned that I'm better with the registers than everyone else was?"

"Maybe you discovered that you are a fast learner and a good trainer?" Caitie suggested.

"Oh. Yeah. I did."

It was painful. But I understood where Drew was coming from. He was only nineteen years old, just a kid, and he was about to be thrown into some adult interviews. I would not have been able to do it at nineteen and it seemed that he was having his doubts as well. The difference between Drew talking about coding and Drew talking about himself in an interview setting was striking. His confidence sank to the floor. His silly and precocious demeanor that played like bravado in the classroom came off as immaturity during the mock interviews. I worried for him. But not more than I worried for myself. Because now it was my turn.

You'll notice, I hope, that I have not exactly been overly boastful about my skills as far as they apply to Tech Elevator. I'm not the best coder and I'm not the fastest learner. Many students like Craig or Fancy or Jack had moments where they said or did something that impressed the entire class into an awed hush. I never had one of those moments. Until the mock interviews.

I killed it. Every question. Just killed it. Do I care that the area of Tech Elevator in which I excelled had nothing to do with computers or logic skills? No. I don't care. I'll take it where I can get it.

"Wow," Caitie said after I had told a third enthralling story in answer to her "Tell me about a time..."

"I don't have any critiques," she murmured as she looked over her notes. "None."

This I took as Caitie's way of saying, "Motherfucker just *gets* it."

But did I just get it? Or was it more that I had prepared way more than anyone in their right mind would for the mock interviews? No one else had ignored a day and half's homework in order to prepare a novella's worth of copy for a fake interview session.

A few days later, Wayne let slip he had experience with HTML and CSS. Some former job he'd worked. He'd been able to finish the homework early because he had done all this before. So, maybe the trick was that there was no trick at all. There was no talent, just grit. No one got it unless they worked their ass off for it.

| Chapter Thirteen |

WE did most of our drinking at a tavern called Beirs. Featuring their own brewed beer (including a porter that I cannot seem to drink enough of), cozy, dim lighting, and remarkable bar food, Beirs is two blocks away from Tech Elevator. The tavern has a second floor that can be rented out for special events and TE had rented it for our halfway party. The drinks weren't free but apps were paid for. Free beer would have been a mess.

Students from previous cohorts were invited to the halfway party. We were Cohort[2], but the cliché programming joke of counting with zero-based numbering was in effect, so there were two classes before us, making Cohort[2] the third of its kind. I drank a couple of porters and posted up with Craig and Bill, talking about a folk singer that Bill was going to see later that night.

We drank and ate while people filtered in around us. I found the former students fascinating. They seemed so knowledgeable, so accomplished. They were living in my future and speaking with them was like being able to pick Merlin's brain. It's not like this with my other profession. I have a friend named Tom who is a writer with a few novels to his credit. Speaking with him about his career, sometimes I feel a hint of jealousy, but mostly I'm just happy that he's found success and I don't relate it to my own journey of writing. The writing industry is so fickle and varied that the idea that Tom and I would travel the same path to publication just isn't realistic. All jealousy lies in the idea that there but for bad luck go I.

But here in front of me, sipping beers and carrying black computer bags that their places of work had given them, were people who had traveled precisely the path that I planned to follow. Every one of the graduates that I spoke with had found a job through the matchmaking process. All of them.

A guy named Slade graduated from Cohort[1] and had been working at FedEx for nearly two months. He admitted that he hadn't done much yet aside from setting up his computer. After acknowledging the slow work, he said, "Oh, you know what? Check this out."

Speaking with Craig and me in the corner of Beirs, Slade pulled out his FedEx-issued laptop. It was different from the ones that TE had given us. It was a PC, like ours, but it looked heavier, industrial, worn. Craig and I stared in covetous stupor.

He folded it open and set it on a round-top table.

"Check that out."

I noticed nothing but a black laptop, sitting precariously below drunk people with wobbling cocktails. But Craig saw it right away.

"Oh yeah," Craig said. "What do they call that? Vorach?"

"Dvorak." Slade corrected.

I still didn't know what they were talking about. I figured it was the type of computer. Craig knew everything about computer makes and models, and I knew nothing.

"I've never tried it," said Craig to Slade, "What do you think?"

"It takes some getting used to, but I'm starting to love it," Slade said. "My project manager swears by the Dvorak setup and he bet the whole team fifty bucks each that if we used it for a month we'd switch permanently."

Like staring at a hidden-picture book, the oddity with the computer finally jumped out at me. The keyboard. It was all wrong.

The keyboard setup you and I are used to is called the QWERTY layout, named after the first six letters in the upper left hand of your keyboard. It's the layout that was drilled into us in high school (or while texting on your phone, if you're under thirty) and it's the layout that the cult of Dvorak says is ruining your life. Created by August Dvorak way back in 1936, the layout was meant to be more efficient than QWERTY, putting the vowels all in one row and common letters right where your fingers sit. Modern-day proponents also claim that it's ergonomic, that your hand strains and carpal tunnel are due to outdated QWERTY.

Slade offered to show us how to set up our computers to handle Dvorak, but I passed. I'm good at typing. Fast. It's basically all I've got going for me. Now was not the time to learn how to do it all over again.

I picked up another porter and floated around the bar a little bit, bumping into people here and there. I recognized a guy named Dev whom I had seen during a presentation but hadn't yet met. Dev worked at CGI, a gigantic contracting company based in Canada with a headquarters in Pittsburgh. Almost a dozen TE grads had been hired by CGI, and Dev was one of them. He visited TE as a representative of CGI when that company visited for a showcase lunch.

We chatted a little bit and Dev explained to me the setup at CGI and, presumably, the setup at many technical contracting houses. After you are hired, Dev told me, they want you to get certified in a number of different things—Java, Selenium, JavaScript. This might take weeks or months. Then, if there is a spot for you, you get assigned to a job, sometimes working from the CGI offices, but often in the field. CGI had people at Giant Eagle, a grocery store in the tristate area, and Sheetz, a large chain of gas stations. But their main Pittsburgh client was FBK National Bank. Over 70 percent of the CGI Pittsburgh Headquarters were doing work for FBK. This was strange for TE grads because CGI and FBK were two of the biggest hiring companies for the program, and both paths usually ended up in the downtown towers of FBK. But the employees rented from CGI tended to make a little bit more cash.

"Have you been assigned anywhere yet?" I asked Dev.

"No," he said, picking up a water chestnut wrapped in bacon. "I've interviewed twice, but no one has hired me."

He went on to explain that CGI employees don't simply get assigned a job and then show up to work. There are openings and the employees of CGI must interview. If they are hired, then the company—FBK, Giant Eagle, Sheetz, whoever—pays CGI the rate that they charge and CGI pays your salary (which is astronomically smaller than the rate they charge). Twice CGI had sent Dev to FBK to interview for a position and twice he had come back to sit on the bench and continue learning.

I was drunk now, so I asked.

"Did you get in trouble?"

As soon as I asked the question I regretted it. Of course he was in trouble. They had been paying him a $65,000 salary for four months and he hadn't earned them even one cent. He was probably gritting his teeth, waiting to get fired any day.

But Dev smiled when I asked the question.

"No," he said simply.

"Well, that's good," I said. I was relieved my faux pas hadn't led to a darker place. "It's cool that they're giving you time to grow."

Dev leaned in. It was sort of weird.

"No one gets fired," he whispered into my ear.

"What?" I asked, taking a healthy step back. "What do you mean?"

"I mean what I said," Dev told me. He looked left and then right, as if he didn't want anyone to overhear what he had confided. I lowered my voice to accommodate him, though I wasn't sure what facilitated the need for secrecy.

"But what if you keep going for interviews and don't get hired?"

Dev had more of a smirk now as he helped himself to the nub of a hot pretzel dipped in dijon. "There are people who have worked for five, six, seven years, who spend ten months out of every year on the bench." He popped the pretzel in his mouth and rubbed his hands together, chewing.

"That's really, *really* nice," I said.

I wasn't sure whether to believe Dev or not. I mean, there was no advantage he obtained by lying to me. But I supposed that he could have formed this half-truth in his head to lessen his own stress about bombing two interviews. If he could maintain the belief that he would be allowed to work the bench ten out of twelve months for the next decade, it lifted a considerable amount of stress from his shoulders. But I didn't know. How could that be?

The next morning I woke up with a bit of a headache and a heavy weight of worry. The students I'd met were interesting people and most of them were friendly and helpful. But the thing that stuck with me the most was that they all seemed to know what they were doing (with the possible exception of Dev). I was eight weeks into the boot camp and I didn't think I was halfway there. I felt like I knew very little and the things I had learned would be impossible to maintain. A sense of dread had set in and it stayed for the weekend.

Mock technical interviews were being conducted the following week and I think this contributed to my shuddering trepidation. The hiring process to get a job as a programmer often has two different interviews—a behavioral interview with an HR person and a technical interview with a lead programmer. The technical interview is often just technical questions. What is CORS? Can you describe a situation where you'd use an interface? What is the difference between unit testing and functional testing? But sometimes there is an actual coding test. There can be an online test where you login from your personal computer and solve two or three coding problems, like the ones we got for homework every day. Then, there was the dreaded whiteboard test.

Whiteboard tests were the boogie man of Tech Elevator. A shiver ran up your back when you heard the phrase and you quickly said a Hail Mary or two to ward off the presence of evil. If it isn't obvious by the name, a whiteboard test is when an interviewer will tell you a coding problem verbally and you must write your answer with a dry erase marker on a whiteboard while they watch.

There are several obvious reasons why this whiteboarding is considered a horror show—you have to work while strangers watch you, you are expected to talk while you do it, explaining your reasoning, you must turn your back to the people in the room, which, I don't know about you, but bugs me out.

The thing is, writing code on a whiteboard is very different from what the students of Tech Elevator had been doing every day for the last two months. We had almost no practice working these problems by hand, all work was typed on a keyboard. Handwriting your code is completely awkward. And the worst part of the awkwardness is that there is no IntelliSense.

Visual Studio is the IDE (Integrated Development Environment) used by the .NET class. I have mentioned before how it course-corrects a coder as they are working. But up until now, I have undersold it. To be clear, I believe Visual Studio to be one of the greatest accomplishments of humanity. And I'm not kidding. I actually got into an argument with Moshe whether the creation of Visual Studio is more impressive than sending a man to the moon. I think it might be. What did we ever get from going to the moon? Moon rocks. What did we ever get from Visual Studio? Google, maybe? I don't know.

Visual Studio makes coding possible for non-geniuses. At least that's how I see it. And even if you don't agree, you have to admit that it makes every coder way, way faster than they would be without it. More accurate too. The way that Visual Studio does this is through a code completion tool called IntelliSense. If you write the name of a variable and then enter a period, a long drop-down list of everything you can do to that variable becomes visible and clickable. Usually with just one or two letters, IntelliSense divines your intentions and serves up your code on a digital platter.

There is no IntelliSense on a whiteboard. The lonely coder, with his back to a room full of strangers, writes the name of a variable followed by a dot and then stares into the snowy abyss waiting for the answer to emerge from his own mind instead of from the depths of the .NET Framework. It's like asking John Henry to race the steam-powered drill. Henry won, you know. But it killed him.

I was still coming into the TE space around seven o'clock for the 9:00 a.m. start. I used this time to work on homework or accomplish the reading from the night before. But with the technical interviews coming up, I figured I should probably get some reps in doodling out problems on a whiteboard.

There were only two or three people in at seven in the morning—me, Kane, the boxer who was living the dream, and Jed, a former operator of big machines who had the work ethic of a Jesuit monk. With the low population, it was easy to secure one of the side rooms with a whiteboard. I poured my coffee, set up in the small room, and combed through homework from previous weeks for a good logic puzzle to draw out.

I was really, really bad at the problems. In my defense, they were not easy.

Around eight o'clock, Matt walked by and saw me working at the whiteboard.

"What'cha doin?"

"Practicing for the technical interviews."

"Cool. Mind if I join?"

"Not at all."

We worked together for about five minutes before Fancy walked by. He stopped and furled his brow. He stuck his head in the door.

"What'cha doin?"

"We're whiteboarding," Matt said. "Come on in!"

So my private study had quickly become a study group. It was OK. We had to take turns, but we could learn while watching the others. Three wasn't bad.

"What'cha doing?"

"Come on in, Craig."

"What's up, my dudes?"

"Hey, Jason. Shut the door behind you."

So now, instead of machine-gunning whiteboard problems, I got a shot every twenty-five minutes or so. The worst part was that everyone in the room was better than me. Some of them stumbled and needed a hint to work out the problem, but most times they thought it through and came up with a working solution. I got my first problem right and completely missed the next two. Not even close. And the one I got right? I was only successful because it was one of the problems I had practiced before anyone else got there. Needless to say, I did not feel good going into the Mock Technical Interview.

The classes swapped teachers to conduct the mock interviews—the Java students got Bill Reeves (.NET Bill) and the .NET students got Bill McDowell (Java Bill). There had been a new teacher hired some weeks into our cohort. She was a database expert who had recently worked for FBK National Bank. Her name was Amanda Gabel, but she quickly became known as !Bill.

The best jokes are the ones you have to carefully explain, so let me do that.

In programming, if you were to say variable A equals five, you would write:

```
var A == 5
```

If you were to say variable A *does not* equal 5, then it would look like this:

```
var A != 5
```

The "!" means that the opposite of whatever follows should be true. So, "not" equal, or more commonly shortened to just "not." So by referring to Amanda as !Bill, we were calling her "Not-Bill." Our teachers were Bill, Bill, and !Bill. Amanda made the joke herself. We all thought it was hilarious.

Java Bill is tall, taller even than .NET Bill. He is bald and wears thick, black glasses, a dress shirt, usually untucked, and jeans most days. Outside of TE, he can be found slightly more casual in T-shirts and flat-brimmed baseball caps. He was just over forty years old during Cohort[2] and had worked during his programming career at CGI, Nike, and Motorola among other places. Along with his degree in Computer Engineering, Java Bill had an MBA. He was known as someone who could help students negotiate once the job offers started rolling in.

Java Bill is wry and quick-witted, his jokes sometimes passing without a laugh because they are too fast or too complicated for the room. He has a streak of Hunter Thompson to him, being astute and curious while eschewing any guilt over a penchant for debauchery. When drinks are happening, Java Bill will have two or three down before anyone else has finished their first. Bill *will* meet you at happy hour. Bill hosts a karaoke every Friday night. Bill threw a parade for himself in New Orleans when he turned forty. So, yeah.

"Welcome to StruggleBus Software," Java Bill said as I entered the room. !Bill sat next to him at the table and smiled. She waved her hand toward the seat where I was expected to sit.

"Struggle...bus?"

Bill pointed to the door. I looked back and saw a sign taped to it. Sure enough, it read StruggleBus Software, a homemade sign with a yellow school bus. I looked back at Bill and !Bill. So, we were going to role play. Great.

Bill explained what StruggleBus Software did as a company, but I was so flustered that I didn't even register it. This wasn't how I thought this was going to happen. I pictured this session as more informational with sentences beginning with, "So an interviewer may ask you. . . " rather than, "Here at StruggleBus, we take software seriously. . . "

Despite my numerous hours logged playing Dungeons & Dragons, I did not do well with the role playing portion. But when the actual questions started coming, I regained my footing. "What are the three pillars of Object Oriented programming?" "How is inheritance different from polymorphism?" "When would you use a static class?"

I knew the answer to all of these. There was a moment when !Bill referred to data structures and I stared at her blankly. Either .NET Bill had never used that term or he had and I had forgotten it. Data structure was a term referring to lists and dictionaries and the like. I knew what they were and could describe them, but stumbled over the vocabulary momentarily. All-in-all, the verbal portion of the technical interview went well.

Bill then took out a deck of cards. On each card was a different coding problem. He shuffled the deck expertly, riffling again and again and then leafing them together, skilled as a Vegas dealer. After a full minute of deft shuffling he looked through ten or eleven cards, negating any work toward randomness that his shuffling had achieved, and picked one that he liked. The performance was vaudevillian in its delivery and totally lost on me due to overwhelming nerves.

"Write a program to find the sum of all odd numbers from 1 to *n*."

"Oh, yeah," !Bill said, nodding in appreciation. "Finding the sum of odd numbers from 1 to *n* is something we do all the time at StruggleBus."

My mind started racing. *OK,OK. That's not that hard. So, it's a for-loop. I have to go through and find all the odd numbers. So I should use "%" on each number and if there is a remainder it's odd, and if there isn't, it's even. Then the ones that are odd, I should add to a total. Should I have an if-statement inside this for-loop?*

And this is how my mind went in the moments after Bill read the question. Then, as I was told to do, I started talking. I verbalized the stream-of-consciousness that was flowing through my brain and at the same time, I started writing my ideas on the whiteboard. I worked for about five minutes, talking and writing, erasing and rewriting.

"And...I think that's it," I said, looking at my work.

"OK..." !Bill said.

"So put a number in for *n* and work it out," Bill said.

I knew I was wrong from their reaction, so I followed Bill's instructions. It quickly became clear that I had left the final answer within the for-loop when it should have been outside the brackets.

"Shit, OK."

"No swearing at StruggleBus."

"Right."

I put the dry erase marker down.

"So would I have failed the test?"

Bill looked at !Bill.

"Do you want us to break character?" she asked.

"Yes," I said.

"What you did would be fine," Bill said. "Of course you want to get the answer correct if you can, but the way you explained your logic—you clearly know what you're doing. If you had been writing at a computer you would have gotten it wrong, saw the error message, and then fixed it. So..."

"Just do a couple of extra problems every day and you'll be fine," !Bill said.

I walked out of the mock technical interview more flustered than when I entered. I appreciated what they said, but was it 100 percent true? I'm sure potential employers would like that I can speak clearly and am friendly. But when all is said and done, they want someone who is good at computer programming. I couldn't believe that, like Dev said, no one got fired from CGI. I couldn't believe that FedEx would hire someone and then not have them do anything for two months. And I couldn't believe that I could miss a coding problem in an interview and still get hired. I would be interviewing for technical positions—skill and knowledge were certainly going to trump any soft skills, right? I needed to get better. And I needed to get better fast. The real interviews started in just seven days.

| Chapter Fourteen |

EACH capstone was built on the last. Following the vending machine capstone we had studied databases. So the second capstone added databases to a command line program. After the second capstone, we studied front end work, so this new skill would be added into our third capstone. The third capstone demanded the background logic from the first, the database access from the second, and a front end. The third capstone was basically a website. We were asked to rebuild the national parks project from the second capstone, but this time it would be a complete application with images and several pages to navigate.

I was randomly assigned to work with Brandon. He hadn't stayed at my house since the weather turned toward spring, but we still talked quite a bit during breaks and I considered him one of my better friends in the class. He still made the drive all the way from Youngstown every day and after nine weeks it hadn't yet broken his will. I was impressed.

We made our plan in the morning of the first day and were coding before lunch. More than anyone else I had worked with, Brandon and I were very close in skill level. If I were to rank the .NET class from one to sixteen, Brandon and I would be an interchangeable seven and eight. We weren't the best coders in the class, but we might have been the two best communicators. For the planning stage, this communication paid off as if one of us was a wiz.

There was no ego and no posturing. We built the MVC structure together. I was a little better at the front end stuff, so I took to importing the images and sizing them reasonably on the page. Brandon had found a way to access the database with half the code, so he went about building our data access layer. We typed and laughed and asked questions of each other and had long stretches of silence where we noodled through tricky logic problems.

I remember the first day of class at Tech Elevator, while typing into a Git window with Rob sitting next to me, thinking that *we were really doing it, we were coding*. This sentiment had been in jest on the first day. Yes, I was legitimately excited about using Git, but I knew I was performing a function of such low-level skill that it couldn't even be called programming. If that Sean could have peered into the future for a glimpse of himself deftly typing out a controller to tie his website together, he would have been floored. If the Brandon and Sean from the first night that Brandon stayed at my house could have seen us buzzing along, they would have headed straight to the Dollar Store with a fist full of ones. We'd come a long way, baby.

We broke at five o'clock, quite pleased with ourselves. For each capstone, at the end of the first day I had gone home in high spirits. But each time, even when I was paired with Jack, there were unsteady waters ahead. The third capstone was no different. I had every reason to worry over what complications we would run into as we drilled down on the details of the project. But I didn't. It had been a good day. When things are going well, I don't like to look for rain clouds. Realism is for people who want to be sad. I spent the night instead in a little cloud of coding euphoria, sipping beers and being fairly full of myself.

Of course I was brought down to earth the next day.

Even though Brandon couldn't get there until close to 9:00 a.m. (remember, he's driving for an hour and a half) I still rolled up to TE at 7:00 a.m. There wasn't a ton I could do because I didn't want to work ahead without Brandon. I clicked around the Tech Elevator handbook, skimming some old chapters.

"Dude, the Reynolds Sportswear coding test is available," Drew said.

"Really..." Matt said, walking up behind Drew and reading over his shoulder.

I stood up, too, and walked over to Drew's desk. We had been waiting for the Reynolds coding test to come through. We weren't allowed to apply for jobs until next Monday, but Reynolds Sportswear had decided that they were going to interview every single student at Tech Elevator.

This was unprecedented. We didn't know how many they were planning to hire. During the previous cohort, the contracting company CGI had gone bananas and hired eight students from a graduating class of just over twenty-five. But CGI had only interviewed twelve of those students. What were the prospects for a company that wanted to talk to every single one of us? How many would they hire—ten, twelve, fifteen? We were giddy with the possibilities, Caitie not the least of us.

A few days before, Caitie had walked into the .NET room with an electric smile on her face.

"Hey, guys, I just want to let you know some really good news. Reynolds wants to have their own matchmaking day!"

When we replied with underwhelmed mutters, she clarified, "They want to come into Tech Elevator and interview *every single one of you*."

That got the reaction she was looking for.

"We don't usually allow this, but they're going to do a coding test first. So, if you want to interview with Reynolds, you'll take the test next week. They're going to send me a link and you'll have to take it by March 18."

She left the room in a hail of applause.

"Why doesn't TE let the companies give a coding test first?" Craig asked me.

"What?"

"What Caitie just said. She said usually they don't do this, but. . ."

"Oh, I don't know," I said.

Jason rolled his chair between us. "Strategy."

"Can you stop rolling your chair between us?" Craig suggested. "We can hear you from the other table. It's, like, two feet away."

Jason continued, nonplussed. "Tech Elevator doesn't want the hiring companies to know which students have the most technical skill. Remember, Kyle said that when reps ask him who his top students are, he tells them they have to interview and find out for themselves."

"Why wouldn't he just tell them?" I asked, though, secretly this pleased me as I was not the best technical student in the class.

"Because TE wants to get the duds hired too," Jason said. "They make their money on having that high rate of placement. If they put out a list of the best scores from one to sixteen, the top ten would get hired and the rest would file for unemployment."

That made sense. Not only did Tech Elevator use that placement percentage as marketing for the company, but the staff bonused big if they hit their placement numbers. The best students in the class were going to get jobs without a problem. The TE staff wanted to do their best to ensure the weakest students were camouflaged, the sheep indecipherable from the wolves. Everyone got jobs and everyone got paid. If some companies hired graduates that actually weren't that great at coding? Well, hopefully they improve on the job.

What this philosophy accomplished, in essence, was to put the Tech Elevator staff squarely in the corner of the student. Everyone, student and staff alike, has the same incentive: 100 percent job placement.

But TE had been enticed into breaking their own rule. They were letting Reynolds Sportswear give each of us an assessment with the promise that every student would be interviewed afterward.

"Where do you click to take this thing?" Drew asked, peering at his email.

"Right there," Matt said, pointing. "But don't click it. It'll be timed. You'll have to take it right now if you open up the page."

"Yeah, I know," Drew said. "I *am* going to take it right now."

It was 7:45 a.m., a little more than an hour before class started. Drew had no idea how long the test would take. He would be surrounded by people while he was working and more and more students would enter the room as we got closer to class time. Everyone told him it was a bad idea, but he clicked the damn link anyway.

It opened up with a series of multiple choice questions. No one had expected this. We guessed the test would contain between one and three coding questions. But, right off the bat, there were ten multiple choices.

"What the hell is CORS?" Drew asked.

"It's shitty beer, right?" Craig said.

"I like Coors," Matt murmured.

"Cross-origin resource sharing," Fancy called out, googling away on his computer.

"What does that even mean?" Drew asked.

"I don't know," Fancy said, looking up, "Is there an answer on the multiple choice that makes sense?"

"Oh. Yeah. Answer C: Cross-origin resource sharing. Thanks, Fancy."

So, for the multiple choice, perhaps it wasn't a bad idea to take the test with half the class looking over his shoulder. It was basically taken by committee, all on Drew's behalf. Everyone helped, no one held back. I assume he got a ten out of ten on the first part, as all of his answers were verified by Google.

The logic problems were another matter.

"Given a date," Drew read out loud, "return the corresponding day of the week for that date. The input is given as three integers representing the day, month and year respectively. Return the answer as one of the following values—Sunday, Monday, Tuesday, Wednesday, Thursday, Friday, Saturday."

It was ten after eight when Drew read aloud the first of two logic problems.

"Any ideas?" he asked.

Crickets.

"Good luck," said Fancy.

The room was quieter after that and we all went back to our own work, looking apprehensively over our shoulders now and then to see if Drew had finished. Brandon came in fresh from the highway and I met him in the Elevate Space to grab a cup of coffee and fill him in on the mess that Drew had gotten himself into.

We talked for about ten minutes, mostly about capstone-related things, and then went back into the .NET classroom.

The place was in upheaval. There were six different conversations going on at the same time. Drew was red-faced and frowning, .NET Bill leaning over his shoulder, studying something displeasing on the screen.

"What's going on?" I asked Craig.

"The Reynolds test," Craig said, clearly flustered. "One test was in C# and the other is in Java."

"What the fuck?" Brandon said.

"Well, one must be for us and the other must be for the Java class," I said.

"I don't know," Craig said, raising his eyebrows. "Bill seems to think we should take both."

"Yeeeeeah..." Bill said, shaking his head. "It says it right there. You have to write in Java for the second answer."

There was a moment of silence and then the class exploded.

I don't know Java!

Does Reynolds know we're a C# class?

I'm skipping it!

Fuck Reynolds!

Does Java use variables?

Craig saddled up next to Bill and asked a much more reasonable question, "So, is this, like, standard in the industry? I thought you usually applied to jobs for specific languages."

"Yeah," Bill said. "Usually on these tests there's a dropdown and you can choose which language to take the test in. But this one says in the instructions to write in both."

"What do you think of that?" I asked.

"I think it's bullshit," Bill said. He shrugged his shoulders and smirked, flipping his long ponytail over his shoulder and loping to the center of the classroom. "All right, everybody—sit down! Take your Socrative Surveys!"

Drew did not take his Socrative Survey. He instead went out into the Elevate Space and did his best to answer a logic question in Java leaning heavily on Stack Overflow.

After a quick pep talk from Bill, we dragged our attention back to our capstones. Brandon and I stared at our screens for a while, but soon we were talking about the Reynolds coding test instead of working. How the hell were we supposed to take a quiz in a language we had never studied?

"I know what I'm going to do," Brandon said. "I'm going to have two computers open and every line I want to write in C#, I'm going to Google how to do it in Java."

"Do you think you'll be able to pass like that?"

"Nope."

"What if you just answer the question with C# and at the top put a comment that you're a C# student? Then, you just write the answer in C#?"

"I don't know," Brandon said. "I guess that could be OK."

I was formulating the idea as I was saying it and I let it stew in my brain all afternoon. This distraction probably added itself to the many reasons why Brandon and I were still at Tech Elevator at seven-thirty that night.

Like I said, the first day of the capstone went fairly well. Brandon and I made all of the different views (web pages that are glued together on the same site) and retrieved all the appropriate data out of the database. The first day was challenging but fun. This second day was just challenging. And long. I had never stayed this late on a Friday night before.

Our problem began and ended with the weather forecast. The user can navigate to a page where they can see a five-day weather forecast with the temperature in either Fahrenheit or Celsius, depending on what they choose from a dropdown menu that we supply. But the rub is, their choice must stick with them for as long as they are perusing the website. For this, we had to write a session.

A session is a piece of code that lets the website remember choices you've made or rights that you have so long as you stay within that session. Think of when you login to your bank account online. You go to XX-bank, you login, and all of your information appears. If you would bring up another browser and go to XX-bank, your information wouldn't be there. It's only on the one where you logged in. Only on the one where you created a session.

Brandon and I needed to create a session where the user chose between Fahrenheit and Celsius and their choice had to stick with them for as long as they were on the website.

We worked on it all day. Like, literally all day. From 9:00 a.m. till around 6:30 p.m. We figured out how to solve the problem, but we never really wrote a session.

Here's what we did: When the user wanted to go to the weather forecast page, we set up a dropdown that made them choose if they wanted Celcius or Farenheit. So far so good. They chose, went on to the forecast page, and checked out the weather in their selected measurement values. The rule of the project was, if they navigated away from the weather and then went back, it should remember their choice. But instead of remembering their choice, we used our Celsius/Farenheit dropdown as a gate to get to the five-day forecast. If the user wanted to go back and take another look at the weather, they chose their temperature metrics again. It wasn't right, not by a long shot, but it accomplished the same thing and no one seemed to notice when they looked over our project. So, we solved the problem.

Really, we cheated. But when you cheat and get away with it, that's called solving the problem. And that's what programming is all about.

Done correctly or not, I was happy to have the third capstone in the rearview. In my mind, I was beginning a shift of priorities.

Up until now, every thought in my head had been about learning and getting better at coding. If something was a distraction, I cast it aside. Things that I had to do, such as the company meet-and-greets and the résumé work, I accomplished but treated it as a second-class task. Now things were changing. This coming Monday, we would be loosed from our chains and allowed to start applying to jobs.

With this paradigm shift, the coding took a back seat and the job search was the primary goal. Before, my mindset was that I needed to learn how to code so that I could get a job. But now I had to find a job, or all the time and money spent learning to code became meaningless. If not used, the skills learned during the four months of the boot camp would fade in the six months following it, like a dream during breakfast. I had the weekend to work on these mental acrobatics and come in Monday fully ready to be an applicant once more.

Actually, I had less time than that. Because I had to take the Reynolds coding test during the weekend.

I fretted over taking the test all day Saturday and in the morning on Sunday. Drew was top three in our class and he scored a 64 percent. Granted, he took the test on a whim and with an audience, but still. Wanting to make sure everything went right, I journeyed to the House of Metal on Sunday to take the test with their reliable wifi and extra monitors.

I arrived around two in the afternoon and there were two or three groups still working on the capstone. They asked me where my group was and I told them I was here looking for peace and quiet to take the Reynolds coding test. Good lucks and empathetic worried looks were given. I filled up a coffee mug and set up shop in the .NET classroom.

No one from .NET was there and I was happy about this. Since I had (basically) finished the capstone, I had forgotten that there might be teams in on the weekend finishing up their work. But luckily, the weekend workers were all Java and so I had the big .NET classroom to myself.

I took a deep breath, opened up the email with the coding test link, and clicked.

I was taken first to the multiple choice test. To my surprise, it was the same series of questions that Drew had received. I thought that the list of questions was random and would shift for each link clicked, but I recognized almost every one of them. I did well. When I closed out that section, I received a nine out of ten.

When the first coding problem appeared, I was again stunned to see that it was the same question that Drew had been asked. *Given a date, return the corresponding day of the week for that date.* A wave of regret crashed over me. I had not expected to see this logic question and so had not memorized an answer to it. I never even talked to Drew about how he approached the problem.

But I was to answer this problem in C#, so I bent my head toward the screen and started typing.

There is a way in coding tests for the testee to enter data into their program and check the work, to put in mock data and see what comes out. This is an essential tool of the IDE for the coding tests. I don't know how I missed the boat, but I didn't know this existed. I should have finished my method and then fed several data into the method to ensure I was receiving the expected results. I needed to know that my logic was sound before submitting my answer. But being a complete neophyte who is sometimes slow on the uptake, I didn't know this was an option. I looked over my work, unsure of how well it would function but unaware that I could test it first, and hit submit.

24 percent.

My heart fell to my toes.

There were some details as to what I had missed and what I had gotten points for, but I was too upset to ingest it. And I still had another logic question to answer. My mind hardened and I felt like I had just received a damning rejection from a publishing house. And so the reaction I had conditioned myself to have over the years rose to the surface. I sipped my coffee and said out loud to the empty room, "Fuck it. On to the next one." I clicked the "Next" button.

In the past, this sentiment was never so literal or immediate. But it helped in the moment.

I took a deep breath and read the black screen. As I scanned the paragraph of the logic question, one word jumped out at me: Fibonacci. I read the whole question just to be sure it was what I thought it was. It was. My fingers itched over the keyboard.

Let's take a step back so I can tell you a little about this Fibonacci bastard. Fibonacci was an Italian Mathematician born in the late 1100s. He popularized a mysterious number sequence that has roots back to the 400s BCE with Indian mathematicians like Pingala, Barata Muni, and other number crunchers who are lost to time. Since he popularized it, it has become known as the Fibonacci Sequence. The number sequence starts with 0 and 1, and then the next number is the sum of the two preceding numbers. So, the first few numbers of the Fibonacci Sequence look like this: 0, 1, 2, 3, 5, 8, 13, 21, 34, 55, 89, 144...and so on for infinity.

The sequence is used in some programming actions, the applications of which I do not understand. But the mysterious part of the Fibonacci Sequence is that it appears in places where it was not purposefully placed, such as metrics in ancient poetry, orchestral music composition, and even in biology, leaf structures on a stem, the petals on a daisy, the structure of a honey bee's family tree. If you would like to link cold, hard logic to the mystic, you can't find a better jumping off point than the Fibonacci Sequence.

At Tech Elevator, this seemingly celestial number sequence is used as a blunt torture device. Early on (much too early, in my opinion), we were given the logic problem to create a method that could count up to any number using the Fibonacci Sequence. So, if I were to feed in the number 65, my method should return 0, 1, 2, 3, 5, 8, 21, 34, 55. The next number in the sequence would be 89, which is greater than 65, so it should not be computed by the method. And my method should work for any number input.

I found this extremely difficult as did the entire .NET class. But it was now familiar. Bill kept drilling it into us and it kept showing up in our homework so eventually we all memorized how to write code to produce the sequence. When I saw Fibonacci show up on the Reynolds test, it was like Batman finding out that the shadowy villain plaguing the city had once again turned out to be the Joker. Batman knows what to do, just punch him in the face and watch out for the poison gas coming from his boutonniere. This being said, I should have been happy to see it included in the Reynolds coding test.

Except, now I had to write the method using Java.

I paused, reading the question over and over. The day before, on Saturday, I had asked my friend Elizabeth if she had ever taken a coding test in two different languages.

"No," she said.

"So, this is abnormal, right?"

"I don't know, maybe," she said. "I haven't had many tests as part of my interviews."

"If you had to answer one question with .NET and one with Java, would you be able to do it?"

"Yes."

The ease and finality of her answer disturbed me. But I pushed on.

"Do you think it would be all right if I just answered in .NET and then in a comment toward the top explained that I answered in .NET because I've never written in Java?"

"Um, I don't know," she shrugged her shoulders. "I guess? I really don't know."

I took Elizabeth's answer as 100 percent permission to use .NET on the entire Reynolds test. Sometimes I just hear what I want to hear.

I had an inkling while writing my Fibonacci answer that what I was doing was absurd, but I didn't stop. At the top of the screen I typed two backslashes, which in programming delineates where a comment begins, and wrote "I have only studied .NET, so I answered using that language."

Zero percent.

The IDE was set up for Java, so my answer did not compute to anything sensible. And that, ladies and gentlemen, is how you score a 38 percent on a coding test.

My first coding test was a complete and utter bombing. I tried to rationalize it away. If a reviewer read the code, they would see that my logic was there, I just had a few small mistakes. I probably got Fibonacci right, just in a different language. I had gotten 90 percent on the multiple choice.

But I knew this was all bunk. Why even have a test if you would accept someone who scored a 38 percent?

This wasn't like scoring poorly on a Socrative quiz. I didn't feel frustrated over the failure. It was sadness, weariness, devastation. It was as if the last eight weeks of Sysophisian work had resulted in me getting flattened by a boulder.

It was a nihilistic walk to the car. I listened to WYEP, my favorite radio station, as I drove from the North Side, across the West End Bridge and into the South Hills of Pittsburgh. In succession they played Gram Parsons, The Cranberries, and the Violent Femmes. It was a jangled mix of music that somehow strung together well. And it really saved the day, like only a good string of songs can.

"How did it go?" Jenny asked as I set my laptop bag down in the corner.

"Looks like I'm not working at Reynolds Sportswear," I said.

We shrugged our shoulders and opened a bottle of wine at four in the afternoon.

| Chapter Fifteen |

THE fateful day finally came. March 18. We were set loose upon the tech career-sphere, allowed to apply to jobs for the first time. After the morning class, Caitie called a Pathway meeting and gave a different kind of speech than she usually gave. Her speeches were of two sorts—instructional (techniques for writing a résumé, tips to have a clear and professional LinkedIn page) or inspirational (stories of how those who came before us persevered, advice on dealing with stress). This speech wasn't exactly one or the other. This one was designed to purely appeal to our logic.

Caitie had a list of interesting stats accompanied by one message: apply to jobs tenaciously. Tech Elevator crunches a lot of numbers on their grads. They have come to some conclusions as to who gets jobs and why. They know who is more likely to get a job and when by gender, education level, skill as a student, and age. These are all things that the students can't control. Even your skill, at this point, was difficult to improve by much. We were in week ten of a fourteen week class. Yes, you were still going to improve, but you probably weren't going to catch up with your competitors (the other students) at this point if you had fallen behind. However, Caitie told us, the variable that matters most we *can* control. Those who apply to more jobs are more likely to get one. And they are more likely to get one quicker. It's as simple as that.

She rattled off these facts:

- Students who applied for an average of one and half jobs a week waited more than two months to find a job.
- Students who applied to three jobs a week found one within one to two months.
- Four applications a week? One month.
- Those who applied to four and a half jobs a week or more were, on average, employed before TE graduation day.

That night I applied to fifty thousand jobs and was hired the day before I sent them.

Not really. That's not even possible. But you get the picture.

Caitie's numbers made sense to me. If we diligently applied to jobs we would have an easier and quicker time finding one. But applying was a complicated business. For one, the applications themselves were often time-consuming. We still had homework, Pathway, and class to think about. Of course, the job-finding efforts outranked everything else, but just because something is outranked doesn't mean it doesn't have to get done. And then there is this: what if you send out ten applications in one day and eight of them come back with a coding test? What if even five or three come back with a coding test? Coding tests can last more than two hours and they have due dates. Each application sent could be the plucked pebble that calls down the avalanche.

So, it wasn't as simple as applying to twenty jobs a day and waiting for the offers to roll in. The more I thought about it, that four and half mark might be something of a sweet spot, a reasonable way to get the numbers on your side without upping your workload to undoable levels. I decided that I would shoot for six or seven applications a week and just deal with the consequences.

After lunch I started searching through LinkedIn and applying to jobs. I already had several job applications that I had teed up for this day. They were filled out and saved on my computer, so I just fired those off and then applied to three more for good measure. One of them rejected me before dinner.

The students knew that the applications were a long shot. That's why you had to send so many. Companies had varying definitions of what an "entry-level programmer" was, and many of them meant people with Bachelor of Computer Science degrees. No one in Cohort[2] had one of these. Caitie advised us to apply to companies even if we didn't meet all the criteria listed in the job posting. She said that these criteria were a wish list, not a set of rules. She said that the tech market was so starved for talent that most were perfectly willing to hire the inexperienced and hope that they grow in skill on the job.

Caitie had given me every reason in the world to trust her, but I still didn't like the odds of me getting a job from filling out an application online. It felt too much like the slush pile, a term from the literary world that meant your book queries were sitting in an email account stuffed with thousands of other queries that might never be read. And, let me tell you, I've been on the slush pile before.

Personally, I was waiting for the matching-making events. We had our first matchmaking next Tuesday, then the Reynolds matchmaking event on Thursday, and then another round of multiple companies the following week. Caitie touted these days as the most likely to get you a job, and most of the former students (literally every single graduate I had spoken with) had found their places of employment on a matchmaking day.

So, did I average more than four and a half applications a week? You bet your ass I did. But I also didn't put a terrible amount of stock in those attempts and looked to the matchmaking schedule as my real opportunities. Besides, I had enough to worry about. I needed to learn JavaScript in the next three days.

The thing is, I thought I had already learned JavaScript. At least a little bit. If you remember, I had studied HTML, CSS, and JavaScript for six months leading up to my time at Tech Elevator. But what I thought was JavaScript was really just me learning the basics of coding. I learned about the different variable types, simple functions, syntax. Kid's stuff.

Real JavaScript is a complicated matter. And .NET Bill is not a fan. His allegiance lies solidly with C#. But this week he found himself teaching a room with sixteen eager programmers bent on warding off the anxiety of the job search with a few hours of coding. Look, we were burned out. On one hand, we felt like we couldn't handle one more lesson or one more piece of homework. But on the other hand, we needed a distraction. Bring on the complications.

Bill didn't often use JavaScript in his professional life. He tried to make a disclaimer at the beginning of the lesson that he was not an expert on JavaScript like he was on C# and databases. Hearing this, I expected him to be hesitant in his teaching, like he had been for the CSS lessons. This wasn't the case at all. Bill might not like JavaScript very much, but he could build an entire website with it in a pinch. And that, combined with his years of teaching experience and natural charisma, was more than enough to teach our pack of newbies.

That being said, there was an element of exasperation in his teaching tone as he discussed some of the rules of JavaScript and their differences with his beloved C#. Bill refers to many of these differences as "Black Magic." He will often insert "Black Magic" in his sentences where "JavaScript" should be. In Bill's mind, JavaScript is mysterious, chaotic code which yields dubious outcomes.

"All right," he'd say, looking at a problem on the whiteboard, "So we'll solve this with a little Black Magic. This isn't C#, ladies and gentleman. Buckle your seatbelts."

I don't claim to fully understand Bill's deep-seated distrust of JavaScript. It seems emotionally charged and personal. Having been in the programming world so long, there is a history between Bill and JavaScript that I don't have the experience to understand. But I do know one of his beefs has to do with the way variables work in JavaScript.

C# is called a "strongly typed" language. You have to declare a number as an "int" before you use it in a variable, you must declare text as a "string." Not so with JavaScript. JavaScript will accept anything as a "var" and try to figure out what the writer intended later, after witnessing the way the variable is used. You can input a wild variety into a "var" variable if you so choose: yes, no, true, false, 5, banana. Doesn't matter. *JavaScript doesn't care!* (Another Bill-ism on the subject of JS).

Whereas in C#, you must tell your methods exactly what variable types they should expect, JavaScript will deal with anything you throw at it. How does it deal with it? Black Magic, of course. It makes assumptions. At the basics, it's an easier language to learn. When things get complicated though, it will often end up doing things you might not have intended.

For example, if you pass two parameters called 2 and 5 and you want to add them together, you might expect to get 7. However, if the parameters happen to be strings (meaning JavaScript sees them as "2" and "5" rather than 2 and 5) and you didn't know, it will concatenate them instead of add them. Your result will be 25. Poof! You've been Black Magicked!

None of this bothered me. I didn't (and still don't) have a deep enough understanding of the way that programming works to see Bill's flaws in JavaScript as a language. My problem came with the architecture aspect that went along with the language.

The way we were taught to build a website using C# was called MVC. We talked about this briefly before. Model, View, Controller. The simple way to think about it is that your View is the front end, what people see, the Model is the back end, the logic and data, and the Controller is the road that links the two together. In this architecture, when the user is on a web page and clicks on a link, then they are sent to another webpage. That makes sense, right? When you're on Amazon and you click on a $35 Weedwacker that you'd like to read about, you are then taken to a details page that will tell you all about the cheap Weedwacker. It works the way you think it works. Both the Weedwacker and the website.

Sites built with JavaScript do things a little differently. Most websites built with JavaScript are single page applications (SPAs). Some of the most popular websites in the world are SPAs—Facebook, Twitter, Gmail. Instead of going to a new page and reloading, the SPA changes right there within the browser. The MVC sites are mansions with a large waiting room (the homepage)—you can choose from several different hallways and explore all the rooms of the house. The single page apps are shapeshifters. You think that you travel great distances, but you never leave the first room. With each click they morph, fulfilling your wildest expectations. And the user doesn't even know. They think they have gone from the homepage to a search list for Weedwackers to a specific Weedwacker's details page, but they've gone nowhere. If MVC is a mansion, single page apps are haunted houses, untrustworthy with their dimensions, dizzying in their trickery.

Whether it was because I was distracted by the job search or burned out from the previous two and a half months of toil, I found the construction of SPA architecture very difficult to grasp. MVC made sense to me—you're here, you click this, you go there. OK. But with the SPAs, we had to deal with event handling and data binding.

Let's stick with the Weedwacker. Say you have your Weedwacker displayed with a picture, a price, and how long it would take to ship. You want to make it so that when a user clicks on the picture, customer reviews appear below. In MVC, you would make the picture act as a link that sends the user the details. But SPAs work with components, not with an array of different pages. The Weedwacker display is its own component. So, if you want to include details when someone clicks on the picture, you have to make an "onclick event" on the picture and then bind it to the reviews data. And then you...

You know what? Fuck it. This isn't worth the effort of explaining.

And that last sentiment is exactly how I felt during the next two weeks of class as we struggled through JavaScript and APIs.

Way, way back, I think it was the second week of class, a panel of Tech Elevator graduates spoke to us about their experiences at TE and their places of work. There were only two graduating classes before us. The old-school students, Cohort[0], had been professionals since the previous fall. The second class, Cohort[1], had only been at their jobs for a handful of weeks. But they all seemed like Greek Gods to us with their calm demeanors and brand new work clothes. We were terrified. Looking upon the gods, it seemed foolish to think that sweaty, worried mortals like us could one day walk among them.

The panelists sat on stools lined in a row in the Elevate Space. Thirty-some chairs had been spread before them and we occupied those chairs with our bodies and our panic attacks. Caitie stood at a podium to the side, smiling and flipping through notecards where she had written questions for the returning graduates. One man, a tall kid with a crew-cut, white T-shirt and black skinny jeans, was asked by Caitie what he thought the most challenging part of his experience at Tech Elevator had been.

Of the panelists, he was the only one who seemed nervous, though I think this was a permanent case with this man and not a condition of situational stress. He talked with his hands in a big way.

"Um, I guess APIs?" he said, making a "W" with his hands.

"OK," Caitie said, prodding him on. "What did you find difficult about learning how APIs work?"

"Well, I just *didn't* learn how they worked," he confessed.

We students laughed nervously. Caitie turned slightly red. Was he knocking the education?

His hands flew about him as he continued to explain, like he was performing a nervous Kata. "I mean, it was the end of the program and I was completely burned out and I was focused on looking for a job and it was like I couldn't focus on anything else and I don't even think I knew what an API was when I showed up for my first day of work."

"Oh, right," Caitie said, "Yes, it can get stressful at the end."

"I mean, I know what an API is now," the graduate assured everyone.

"OK," Caitie said, shuffling her cards, ready to move on.

"I *make* APIs now," he squeezed in, his arms outstretched like Jesus on the cross.

At the time, I thought to myself, *No way. I understand it's going to get hard, but I will* not *zone out. I will be focused and present until the last day of class.* And I meant it. And I tried to do just that. It didn't work out the way I intended.

I was now at the exact point of class as this alum had been and the exact same symptoms were happening to me. My brain power had whittled away, like my thoughts were a cupboard raided by mice in the night. The main culprit was definitely the job search. I checked my email for replies from applications every ten minutes. And if there was an hour where several different things needed to be done at once, job-searching always outranked figuring out how an API worked. But there was another symptom, too, which was much more insidious.

During class, there was nothing to do but pay attention to Bill. The screen on my computer was angled toward the front of the class, so he would see if I was searching for jobs or checking my email. Not that Bill would have called me out on it, but it would have been rude, so I never did it. With no option for tomfoolery, I focused completely on the lecture during the allotted class time like I had for the entire cohort. But my mind at the end of March was not like my mind at the beginning of January. In January, I turned a hyper-focus Bill's way and breathed in each sentence like its contents were keeping me alive. Now, I applied the same hyper-focus, but the results were a jumbled mess. Bill would say something like, "API stands for Application Programming Interface. Think of an API as a warehouse that you can call on from your website to deliver the data where and when you need it."

Those sentences make sense. Bill has told the class what the letters API stand for and then given an apt metaphor to understand what an API does. But in my head the sentences were chaotic. I heard each individual word, unable to group them together as a thought.

Think. API. Warehouse. Deliver. Need.

I knew all those words and each of them meant something to me. But any time I tried to internalize what one of Bill's sentences meant, the words were small islands on the ocean, connected only beneath opaque waves.

Data. Call. Website. Interface.

Word soup. Unlike the young man from the panel, I *did* know what an API was upon graduating Tech Elevator. But if we wanted to talk about it beyond its textbook definition, I was lost. I wondered with creeping dread whether anyone during next Tuesday's matchmaking days would want to delve into the topic of APIs.

| Chapter Sixteen |

BEFORE the matchmaking event, we filled out a survey telling Caitie which companies we wanted to interview with. There was not enough time for every person to interview with every company; it simply wasn't tenable. There were certain companies that were more popular than others—a small software company called Single Source had given an inspiring presentation some weeks back and the mammoth contracting company CGI had hired eight TE students from the last cohort, making them seem particularly attainable. These two companies were on nearly everyone's list and Caitie had the unenviable job of deciding who got a seat at the table.

I didn't request Single Source, but I did request CGI. Single Source was intriguing, but they scared me off because I believed they planned to dig deep during the technical interviews. Before filling out Caitie's company survey, I had taken another online coding test and it greatly affected my choices. I had applied to work at a large law firm and after reviewing my résumé, they sent me an online coding test. I bombed it terribly. Just like the Reynolds test.

I talked to Bill early in the morning when I arrived at the House of Metal.

"I keep failing these coding tests. I just can't do them."

Bill was perplexed. "Why? What's the problem?"

I didn't have an answer to that question. There were other students who were holding their own on the coding tests. Most people failed the Reynolds test, but some didn't. Craig commiserated with me about how difficult the Reynolds test had been, but he didn't share what his final score was, which led me to believe that he probably performed well. At my current skill level, I could speak convincingly about how programming worked and I could solve most basic coding problems. But when it got beyond that, I drowned. I didn't want to subject myself to the Single Source interview. I felt like I would be wasting their time and that I would be depriving myself a shot at a place that might actually hire me.

Not confident in my skills, I went for the companies that I thought were going to hire a lot of people. The two places I really wanted to work were CGI and FBK Bank. Both companies had made presentations at TE and both had sent charismatic, inspirational people. Also, they were both unfathomably large companies that could scoop up plenty of software developers whenever they wanted. These were my top two, and I chose three other companies that I was less excited about but still one thousand percent willing to work at.

I was concerned that I might not get my top picks. Every student I talked to also wanted to interview with CGI, and FBK seemed to be a popular choice as well. Caitie had said that those who had attended all Pathway events would have preference over those who did not. Not only had I attended all the Pathway events, but I had gone to several optional workshops as well. I was also one of only a handful of students who had actually gone to a networking event. I only went to one and I found it basically worthless, but still. Kudos, please.

I shouldn't have been worried. When the schedule posted, I had every single one of my picks. There were others who were not so lucky. There were students who were dead-set on working for CGI who did not get a chance with them at matchmaking. Caitie had set it up so that these students could apply outside of matchmaking, their résumés sent in a batch from Tech Elevator so that they received special attention, but it wasn't the same. Caitie was in a tough spot and it was a balancing act to keep all the students calm.

Even with me, who had gotten everything I asked for, there was worry. The matchmaking at Tech Elevator was the big kahuna. This was why you were here. This was where you were going to get a job. I tapped on the desk in front of me with a pen while looking over my interview schedule; I had three interviews on Tuesday, one with Reynolds Sportswear on Thursday, and then two more interviews the following Tuesday. Only six shots? I guess in my head I thought there would be something like ten or fifteen interviews. When I send out query letters trying to sell a book, I send somewhere between fifty and seventy communications.

Six interviews. Each one seemed fragile and precious.

And then suddenly there were no longer six.

It started as a rumor: Reynolds was no longer interviewing every TE student on their matchmaking day. The sour looks and frantic, furtive conversations between the staff seemed to confirm it, but I didn't believe it until I heard it from Caitie's mouth.

"They've decided to just choose *some* of the applicants to interview rather than the entire cohort," Caitie told us.

"But didn't they say it didn't matter what the scores were on the coding tests? That they would interview everyone? That they were looking for people who could grow with the company?"

"They did," Caitie said with thoughtful deliberation as she discussed a valuable business partner's indiscretion, "but it seems like their goals may have changed."

"They pulled the ol' switcheroo!" Bill declared when we pestered him about it. "They wanted to see the goods before they bought."

It was apparent to me that the Tech Elevator staff was not happy with this turn of events, but they were trying to play it cool because they thought that Reynolds might still hire a large portion of our class. As far as I can tell, it went down like this: Reynolds wanted all the students to take a coding test and Tech Elevator had told them that was against their policy. If Reynolds wanted to be involved in the matchmaking event, they would interview first and then put their selected applicants through whatever rigamarole they wanted afterwards. The TE director, Kyle, led these discussions. In his point of view, the coders that TE produces are unique in that they come from different walks of life. Many of the students have customer service in their background, which might seem trite but is actually an indicator of strong communication skills, something a software manager would be willing to pay to have on his team, even if the technical skills might be weaker than average. Also, these students have run the gauntlet of the coding boot camp. A boot camp graduating class is a group of people who just worked their asses off for an extended period of time. They're in a groove and they're going to keep grinding. If they're not great at writing JavaScript now, just give them three months on your payroll and see what happens. And lastly, you can pay them less. A twenty-two-year-old computer science graduate coming into his first entry-level job can hope to make high $60,000s, low $70,000s. TE's average salary that they used in their marketing wavered around $60,000. So, yes, a college graduate with a computer science degree might have better technical skills than a boot camp graduate. However, they might not be able to talk to their coworkers in a manner conducive to business; they might be young, lazy, and entitled, as many of us are coming out of college, and you have to pay them ten to fifteen thousand dollars more a year. Boot camp grads might not be a good fit for every company, but they are a good fit for many.

The strong belief of Tech Elevator is that if there is an interview first, the student's pluck and perseverance will have a chance to shine. These attributes might be shuffled aside by an impersonal online coding test, which could vary wildly in difficulty-level depending on what service the company uses to supply its test. The student would miss out on an opportunity and so would the company.

Either Reynolds didn't buy what Kyle was selling or they were just being stubborn. They wanted the test first. They pressed the issue, saying that they would still talk with everyone and that they might hire a lot of students. TE caved; they made the exception for them. Then, when many of the scores came back lower than expected, Reynolds decided to only interview a selection of the applicants. Whether they had premeditated this move or whether they were shocked by some of our low scores and changed their minds, it's hard to say. And, really, it's their company. It's their time to spend, their prerogative to do as they wish. There were no contracts signed about this. I can definitely see the Reynolds side of the argument. Why waste time interviewing applicants you know you will not hire? But I can say, whether right or wrong, that Cohort[2] at Tech Elevator felt betrayed and I think the staff did as well.

No matter how many times we asked, Caitie would not tell us who Reynolds was interviewing and who was getting screwed.

She claimed she didn't know yet and maybe she didn't. Caitie is a consummate professional and I think she wanted to break the news the right way, not blabbing to a room-full of students or coldly posting a schedule for the Reynolds matchmaking day for us to race toward like the kids in a high school musical, hoping for a lead role but instead being carted off to the chorus.

I never answer my phone if I don't recognize the number. Who does that? So I let Caitie's call go to voicemail.

"Who was that?" Jenny asked as I listened to the voice mail.

"It's Caitie."

"From Tech Elevator?"

"Yeah."

"Do you think maybe one of the companies you applied to contacted her?"

"Mmm, I don't think so," I said.

I guess part of me hoped it was some type of surprise good news, but I knew what was up as I returned her call.

"I'm so sorry, Sean, but your name was not on the list of students that Reynolds wants to interview."

"No, I figured that would be the case," I said. "My score on the coding test was terrible."

She seemed like she wanted to say more and that she was holding her tongue. We ended the call.

Honestly, I wasn't that broken up about it. I had a lot of anxiety about the Reynolds interview. I felt like I would be defending my shitty coding test score the whole time and that no matter what I said I wasn't getting the job. And there were a few other reasons too. After some consideration, I was pretty sure I wanted to work downtown. The Pittsburgh public train system is not very convenient for most of the city, but I happen to live in a perfect spot with a stop right by my house that travels straight to the center of downtown Pittsburgh. If I worked at Reynolds I would most likely spend two hours commuting everyday. I don't like driving. I don't like cars. I had a far-off fantasy of securing a job downtown and selling our second vehicle.

Plus, there was the weirdness with the Reynolds field trip we had taken the month before. The students who had lost their interviews got together and shared a bowl of sour grapes. There was a rehashing of the harassment we all witnessed during that field trip and there was a general consensus that Reynolds Sporstwear could go fuck themselves.

The people who still had interviews with Reynolds stayed out of these bitch sessions. No one held it against them that they were still eager to work for the company. We all knew if the shoe was on the other foot, that our high morals would vanish and we would be trying our damnedest to secure a job there. I mean, we're human. There was a gym and a basketball court on the premises.

My focus shifted to CGI and FBK National Bank. Both had offices in downtown Pittsburgh and both companies had sent representatives to Tech Elevator whom I clicked with. It was hard to prepare for CGI since they were a consulting firm and a programmer could end up working in any number of different places. FBK was a different story. They had a website I could pour through and question. Also, we had the inside track that the jobs FBK was hiring for were mainly in the realm of automated testing.

I was completely sold on FBK from the moment I met Hank from their Testing Center of Excellence, and then later Zoe and Meghan. The truth is, I didn't know what I wanted to do in the world of software. Not really. So instead of looking for a company whose product or work interested me, I looked for people that I liked. And I liked these three. They came off warm and friendly, but with an air of sophistication that both the representatives of CGI and Reynolds did not possess. I wasn't looking for cold professionalism, a vibe that I got from the people at BNY Mellon and FedEx. But I wanted something inherent in my relationships with these companies that solidified the fact that this would be a career. The people from both CGI and Reynolds were funny and frank, almost irreverent at times during their talks with us during their showcases. This attracted a lot of the students. Maybe it's because I was older than many of my schoolmates, but I was most drawn to those who could strike the balance between human compassion and professional distance. Maybe I'm just no fun.

And, to be clear, I would have taken a job from *any* of these companies. Let's not act like I wasn't desperate. But during these days, any downtime at TE was spent discussing which company you most hoped to work for, so there was some splitting of hairs, like getting in the weeds about which celebrity you most want to sleep with.

The desperation started closing in on me as I got dressed on the morning of March 26. It was matchmaking day. I had gone out and bought new clothes for the occasion with money I did not have. Shopping at Macy's, I bought a new yellow tie that I really liked. But I had also saved a few bucks by buying dark gray pants to go with a light gray suit jacket that I already owned. Wearing it that morning, I wasn't so sure about my choices. I have some opinions about suits. I don't like when the material of the suit jacket is the same material as the suit pants. I think it looks like a costume, akin to a referee or a delivery person. I know I am in the minority in this thinking and that having the same color suit jacket as the pants is, in large part, what defines a "suit." But monochromatic clothing just doesn't do it for me.

However, standing in front of the mirror that morning, I wondered if selecting a gray suit jacket with slightly darker gray slacks had been a smart choice. But it was too late. I had bought my clothes, now I had to interview in them.

I was nervous almost to the point of paralyzation during the drive to Tech Elevator. Like I said before, I had not done a ton of interviewing in my life. When you stay at a company for sixteen years, you tend to let your interviewing skills slide. I had *conducted* many interviews on behalf of Barnes & Noble, and I thought that this experience would come to bear. I don't think I had ever prepared for an interview like I did for the three I was driving toward, and there was part of me that was sure this would pay dividends. But it was still terrifying. So much depended on the next several hours.

I saw that everyone was in the Java classroom, so I hung a left to join them instead of going straight to the Elevate Space like I normally would.

Sitting in his wheeled desk chair, Jason rolled backwards into my path.

"What's up, my dude?"

My first interview wasn't until 3:30 p.m. and I thought I was being a spaz by showing up at 1:00 p.m. Jason had been there since 9:00 a.m. He explained the setup to me.

Kyle's office, the Bills' office, the downstairs meeting room and the study rooms were all filled with interviewers from different companies. Several long tables had been set up in the .NET classroom. There were two companies at each table conducting interviews and the Elevate Space had the same layout with still more companies for the matchmaking event. There were snacks in the Java classroom and board games to occupy us as we awaited our turn on the interview ride.

I put my bag down in the corner, checking the mirror that was provided to make sure that the windy walk from my car to the House of Metal hadn't given me a wispy mohawk. As I tamed my mane, Drew entered the Java room with a bang.

His hair was a mess, cowlicked on one side, smashed into the flat shape of his mattress on the other. He wore a blue pinstripe suit, a red tie, and a white, wrinkled dress shirt with a large, obvious, yellow stain just to the left of the tie. Drew never looked tidy, exactly, but he seemed particularly disheveled upon his entrance to the Tech Elevator matchmaking day, like a comedian who has just done a quick costume change in preparation for his salesmen sketch. The first thought I had was *How did his mother let him out of the house looking like that?* and the second was that this might be some form of self-sabotage.

Glasses akimbo on his smirking face, he made a round of the Java room, shaking everyone's hand and saying "Tell me about a time. . . " as a greeting, in sarcastic reference to Caitie's HR interview questions that had haunted us since mid-February.

This joke spread like measles. Everyone was shaking hands and saying "Tell me about a time" throughout the rest of the matchmaking process.

"Dude, you look terrible!" Jason said to Drew. "What are you doing?"

Given the state of Drew's appearance, one might have expected Drew to shrug his shoulders to Jason's remark and say "Who cares?" How could he look this ridiculous and not be aware? But Drew's face flushed red, the smile fell from his lips and he looked down at his attire, blindly searching for something amiss.

"What'd you mean? I look great."

He used the same deadpan delivery that he liked to joke around with, but this time it was bluster. He was the only person in the room who had been shocked by what Jason said. Drew spent the next twenty minutes in the bathroom wrestling with his hair and trying to get the stain out of his dress shirt.

The truth was, Drew had less to worry about than the rest of us. The nineteen-year-old phenom had the curious talent of securing interviews without Caitie's matchmaking connections. His LinkedIn page received hundreds of views a week, whereas the rest of us were getting five and six. He had had three interviews since March 18 and had been the first to actually get a job offer. The offer was for front end development and it paid $55,000. He turned it down.

He turned it down!

Though Drew thought he could make more money, the main reason he turned it down was because he would be the only developer in the company. He would have no one to lean on, no one to ask questions of, no one to act as mentor. It was an astute and mature decision, really. Yes, the money was slightly less than what TE grads were averaging in Pittsburgh, but having lived for sixteen years at or below the $40,000 salary, I had some wild ideas about what $55,000 a year meant. I can't see that, given the same spot, I wouldn't have yelled "Yes!" and jumped foolishly into the deep end.

I sat down on a couch and looked over my notes. I had memorized my work stories to the point that I could rattle them off smoothly, but it had become an obsession over the last week to read them again and again, changing little words here and there. Before I got too far, Christopher sat down with me.

"I'm next," he said, with the finality of a funeral director.

He sort of looked like a funeral director too. In a good way. He had a really nice suit, perfectly fitting and all black.

"How are you feeling?" I asked.

"Terrible. I feel like I'm being swallowed."

Christopher was also a writer, the only other writer in the class, as far as I knew. He claimed to have written a novel over a thousand pages long. I believed him.

"You'll do fine," I said.

"I look like a child," he replied.

"No..."

He did look very small in his suit. The perfectly tailored fit highlighted his thin frame. He couldn't be more than a hundred and twenty pounds, I imagined. But with the earnestness of a mob of poets.

"It's five minutes to two!" Caitie called from the doorway of the Java classroom. "Everyone with 2:00 p.m. interviews, please line up!"

"Good luck, Christopher," I said.

"Thank you," he replied, breathless and defeated.

Caitie was in a state of manic, organized glory. Always positive, she seemed completely primed and blissful today, like an NFL player running out of the locker rooms on Sunday. She carried a clipboard with a detailed schedule of who was interviewing in which room at what time. She went down the line of students making sure that each person was accounted for.

"Steven, you're in Kyle's office with Single Source."

"Wayne, you're in the green room with National City Bank."

"April, you're in the .NET classroom with Synergy."

"Christopher, you're in the Bills' office with FBK."

Hut!

And then she moved away from the door and they all deployed, like paratroopers out of a plane, screaming into the night.

Anxiety nearly overwhelmed me as I watched them go. My interviews started in an hour. And when they started, they were rapid fire. I had FBK at 3:30 p.m., then a half hour break, then CGI and Plus Consulting back-to-back from 4:30 p.m. to 5:30 p.m. I chatted with Craig a little bit but we really didn't have anything to say to each other. I stared blankly at my notes.

"It's three-thirty!" Caitie called. "It's three-thirty! Three-thirty interviewers please line up at the door!"

Like barnyard animals when they sense feed will be thrown, we waddled our way dumbly to the door and lined up for Caitie. I clutched tightly my notebook and pen.

"Craig, you're in the downstairs office with CGI."

"Joe, you're in Kyle's office with Single Source."

"Diane, you're in the white room with Plus Consulting."

"Sean, you're in the Bills' office with FBK."

So my number one pick was also my first interview. I was being interviewed by Zoe, an HR representative, and Meghan, the head of FBK's automated testing center. I had met each of them previously. FBK had three times sent representatives to speak with us as part of one event or another. I had had a good conversation with Zoe where I felt I made a connection, but I had only spoken with Meghan superficially. Caitie seemed very taken with Meghan as an employer and, in my estimation, spoke more highly of her than she did some of the other companies.

"Hello," I said as they rose from their seats to shake my hand. There was a chair for me to sit and the women were in two opposing chairs a few feet away. There was not a desk between us.

The interview started with Meghan detailing what the Testing Center of Excellence (TCoE) was doing at FBK. Meghan wove a story of a bank bogged down with old habits, slow to adopt new tech. She spoke with disdain about manual testing and renting employees from consulting companies rather than hiring talent. She talked of the need to build in-house rather than buying software. And at the center of everything was automation. The word was like gospel in the mouths of the FBK representatives.

That said, much of the conversation was about communication and work ethic. I was able to use some of my stories to answer their questions and the ease with which I told the stories, borne from the obsessive work I put into constructing them, enabled the conversation to flow easily. The highlight of the interview came when Meghan inquired about my being a writer. This made me queasy.

I had never claimed that I am a writer on a résumé before, even though it's how I primarily spent any time outside work since the age of twenty. I have published five short stories in literary magazines, self-published one novel, and had one novel published by a small press, but the small press was created and run by friends of mine, twins whom I grew up with named Bob and Brad Simon. In my head, I've always thought of writing as an *attempted* career and not a real one. You can support yourself with a career. My nearly twenty years of writing probably could have supported me for three or four months, financially.

But Caitie had convinced me to include the writing on my résumé and when I was hesitant she convinced me some more. So, it was on there. And now I had to talk about it in a professional capacity. Nowadays, I'm getting better, but I often get very awkward when I have to admit to someone that I write. I've penned ten novels and I still feel like a liar when I tell someone I'm a writer.

"Novels," I said in answer to Meghan's question about what I write. "Mostly fantasy for adults and children. But I've written other types of fiction too."

And then a sudden inspiration hit me, an idea that had not been written down in my notebook in preparation for this interview. I diverged from the comfortable path I was on and bounded heedlessly into the unknown.

"I've actually found that writing a novel and writing software have a lot of similarities," a voice said from my mouth.

Meghan and Zoe raised their eyebrows.

"How so?" Meghan asked.

"It's the challenge of the big project. You can't sit down and write a novel in one day. You have to break it down into chunks and get each piece to work separately and then string them together to form something cohesive. You have to work on the novel a little each day, slowly building into something that looks like a story. Working on an app is the same way. You have to start with the concept, the architecture, and then fill that in slowly with all the components. And, sometimes, halfway through, you might realize the original plan you made could be better another way, so you have to pivot, change your plans, refactor. Things won't always go right and you have to be ready to scrap work, save what you can, and start building again toward your goal. Both the novel and the app take patience, creativity, and focus stretched over a long period of time."

I can't overstate how well this went over. Zoe, who hadn't really said anything throughout the interview, whispered, "Wow. . . "

Meghan nodded her head. "Yeah, I can really see how that's true."

The conversation continued, but I could tell I had scored some major points. When the half-hour interview ended, I floated back to the Java classroom elated.

| Chapter Seventeen |

I was so high from my interview with FBK that the following interviews with CGI and Plus Consulting were something of a blur. They went well, particularly the CGI interview, but I tried to shoehorn my philosophizing about how novels were like software in both conversations and it did not play as well as it did with FBK. I thought that I did well with CGI but that the Plus Consulting interview was awkward. I had good moments in all three interviews and with my penchant for wishful thinking, I more than half expected calls for second interviews from all of them.

The next day, Reynolds Sportswear was coming in to interview the chosen students. On the drive in that morning I felt a light sense of relief that I was not one of these students. Mentally, I had turned so hard from the company that I thought I didn't care at all. I told myself that I was glad I wouldn't be working at Reynolds. It was a little different when I walked into the .NET classroom.

I set my computer bag down at my space next to Craig and looked around. Craig was wearing his interview clothes. So was Matt. And Jason and Fancy and Diane and Jack.

Drew entered the room in his messy suit. "Tell me about a time," he said to Jack, shaking his hand.

"Tell me about a time," Jack replied with less enthusiasm, looking worriedly at his notes.

They had all done well enough on the Reynolds coding test to be asked to interview. Wearing a T-shirt and jeans, I sat down and opened my computer, checked my email, surfed the job boards, glazed over while staring at LinkedIn.

Derrick entered the room wearing his black and white suit. I was hollow. The interview attire was a direct line in the sand. Those wearing them were better coders than those who weren't. That's the way it was and no amount of wishful thinking could change that.

Brandon came in from his commute from Youngstown, grinning, resplendent in baggy jeans.

"You all have interviews with Reynolds?" he asked the suited up students. "Damn, I bombed that shit."

He laughed and began to unpack his computer. "Well, Bill's teaching the rest of us Bootstrap today while you all are trying to get *jobs*, so good luck being a software developer and never knowing Bootstrap."

Before Brandon had come into the room, I applied to two jobs and was working on a third application. His flippant attitude made me stop. I took a breath and tried to calm down.

"Good luck today," I said to Craig, because I realized I hadn't said that yet.

"Thanks, man" he said. "Take some notes on Bootstrap for me."

"Will do."

There are plenty of what are called "frameworks" for programming. .NET is a framework for the C# language. Using a framework with a particular language abstracts some portion of the difficulty and tediousness of writing software. Instead of creating everything from scratch, someone has prewritten certain generic choices that the programmer can choose and customize. Good frameworks can make a coder faster and more free from mistakes.

Because frameworks generally make programming less of a pain in the ass, there are many frameworks that deal with the biggest pain in the ass of all, CSS. At the time of my boot camp, Bootstrap was the most popular framework for front end work. Developed by programmers at Twitter, Bootstrap makes front end easier, with a focus on mobile, cool-looking buttons, and clean, properly-spaced forms. It takes the greased-up-crocodile that is CSS and tames it, cows it under your power.

Since there were students interviewing for Reynolds from both the .NET and Java classes, .NET Bill taught the Bootstrap lesson in the Elevate Space rather than one of the classrooms. These lessons in the main room were always a little different because there was no whiteboard. The whole lesson consisted of Bill's projected computer screen. Also, it was understood that this one-off display would have no homework accompanying it, which made a big difference to the level of intensity with which we all paid attention. For me, lack of homework aside, it was impossible to pay attention once the interviewers arrived and I heard the applicants begin to introduce themselves.

It was a painful scene. About twenty of us sat in front of Bill on folding chairs with notebooks in our hands. All of us had done poorly on the coding test and the consequence of that was playing out audibly behind us as Craig told his interviewer it was nice to meet him and went into the white room to talk more privately.

The rest of the Bootstrap lesson passed in jealous turmoil. I didn't retain much and my note-taking stopped. When it was over, I had missed the last twenty minutes of information. I felt pretty rotten as I slouched back to the .NET classroom, thinking, for the first time since I started the cohort, that I might call it a day and go home even though I had still work to do.

I opened up my email and saw a new message from Zoe, the recruiter from FBK. I had written thank-you emails to all of my interviewers and they had been slowly responding all day. The responses were meaningless, most of them just saying thank you back to me or that it was nice to meet me. But still, it felt good to receive a communication that wasn't a rejection. Zoe's email started out the same way as the others.

Thank you very much for your kind email, it read in reply to my thank-you.

OK, business as usual.

I will share with you that we very much enjoyed the conversation with you, it continued.

Mmm. OK, that's good. And a little more than standard.

...and are very interested in further conversations.

YES! THAT'S A SECOND INTERVIEW!

And then there was a space and a line that I could have easily missed in my excitement.

Do you have some time this afternoon to connect?

I read the email three hundred times.

I replied saying that I was free all day and she replied suggesting 2:30 p.m. as a good time to talk. She would call me. At 2:30 p.m.

Craig entered the Elevate Space and sat down next to me. I was shaking with excitement.

"How did it go?" I asked, doing my best not to forget the fact that he actually just finished an interview. I had the inclination to steamroll over whatever he was about to say and blurt out that I was going to get a second interview with FBK.

"Um, I don't know," he said, frowning and tilting his head to one side. "I think it went pretty well? It was technical for sure."

"Were you stumped at any point?"

"No. I mean, the conversation moved along OK, I guess. I do wonder how many people they're looking to hire."

"Why?" I asked.

"I don't know. I mean, at the beginning it was like, Reynolds is going to hire everybody—but now, I don't know. It wasn't an easy interview."

We chatted a little more about his morning. Craig tends to underplay everything. As the details came out, it started to sound like he had done pretty well. And according to what Craig relayed, I think I would have gotten clobbered in the Reynolds interview.

"So how was Bootstrap?" he asked, when we had exhausted his interview.

"FBK is going to have me for a second interview."

"Whoa! Cool!"

We read the email together, discussing each word like it was Proustian prose.

"So, you're going to talk to her today?"

"Yeah, at two-thirty."

"What do you think she wants to tell you?"

"Oh, I don't know. She probably wants to describe the position more fully, make sure it's what I think it is. Maybe set up a date for the second interview."

"I mean..." Craig paused, reading the email silently. "You don't think she's going to straight-up offer you the job, do you?"

"No..."

Yes. Yes, I did think that!

"Hmm," Craig said, finally pushing away from my computer and flipping open his own. "Well, good luck, man."

"Thanks."

"She's totally offering you that job," Jenny said on the phone.

"I don't know," I said, grinning. "I'm not really sure why she would want to talk. If it's just to set up a second interview, she could just do that over email."

"You can't say 'yes' right away," Jenny told me.

"What do you mean?"

"I mean, if she makes you an offer, you have to tell her you're going to think about it. I want to discuss it before you agree to anything."

"Even if it's for, like, one hundred thousand dollars a year?"

"Even then."

As you can see, I built up this phone call quite a bit in my head.

"Hi, Sean, thanks for taking the time to speak with me," Zoe said.

"HELLO!!!"

I might have been shouting.

We talked a bit about the boot camp and what type of assignments we were currently working on at Tech Elevator. Then Zoe launched into a description of the TCoE (Testing Center of Excellence) at FBK and all of the strides they were making with automated testing. After she was finished with her description, she asked me if all of that sounded good, sounded like the type of thing I would enjoy doing, and I said yes. Then she told me that she didn't have a date yet, but that there would be a day for second interviews at the FBK headquarters downtown. They would send out all the second interview emails on the same day and the students would come as a group. She assured me that I was part of this group.

No job offer. When I hung up the phone I only felt crestfallen for a moment. Just a moment. But in that moment there was the exhaustion of being on a long trail home where you think you have found a shortcut only to realize you have so much more to go. It was good that I got the second interview, but I still had to actually participate in that interview. I still had to perform, still had to be on and sharp. And also, since the FBK job wasn't in the bag, I had to keep sending out résumés and study for the two additional matchmaking interviews that were coming up the following Tuesday. A job offer on March 27 would have saved me a hell of a lot of work.

I tried to play it cool, but I did drop it in conversation here and there that I received an email from FBK. Craig had not heard anything back from them and, as far as I could tell, neither did anyone else. So why was I the only one?

Walking by Caitie's office, I saw her packing up for the day. I stuck my head in and said "hello."

"Hey, I just wanted to let you know that I received an email from Zoe."

"That's great," she said, her face lighting up.

"Yeah, I talked with her too."

"Really?"

I pulled out my phone and showed Caitie the email. She nodded, smiling. She looked at me once again like she wanted to say something but was holding back.

"What?"

"They really liked you," she said.

"That's good."

"It is. They really, *really* liked you."

Then she stared at me weirdly as if she was screaming telepathically. Or maybe I imagined it.

That night Jenny and I stayed up late examining all the angles of the interview, the email, the phone call, and Caitie's enigmatic insistings.

That Thursday, things started to get dramatic at the House of Metal. Rather than students playing competitive ping pong or drinking beers on the roof at shamefully early hours in the afternoon, the place had gone quiet. People were in the stairways crying in solitude, heads were being held in hands in the Elevate Space, conversations were as brief as astronauts on a doomed spacecraft, trying to conserve oxygen. The students of Cohort[2] were freaking out.

I was not the only student to get a callback in the forty-eight hours since the matchmaking ended. CGI had invited students to second interviews as had Single Source and Plus Consulting. Reynolds had even sent out some feelers, though no dates were set for second interviews. I was the only one whom FBK had contacted and I would be lying if I said this didn't give me a certain sense of glee.

Some people were more forthcoming with their callbacks and some kept it closer to the vest. Brandon acted as something of a social collector of information. As I've said previously, one thing I have in common with Brandon is that we both love to talk about money. Well, I can extend that statement to also add that we have no shame in asking people about their annual salary. We do not understand the stigma that makes salaries a private thing. I know that this is a stereotype of a tacky person, and I am guilty of being that person. I agree that asking your lawyer brother-in-law what he makes a year is nothing more than nosiness. But asking someone within your own career-path should be free of this stigma. We can all help each other negotiate and make sure no one's getting underpaid. That's just business, folks.

Over the next few weeks, my coffee chats with Brandon turned into a listing of who had gotten a callback to which company, when their second interview was, and speculations on what that company might pay them. Brandon was an encyclopedia on these matters. Students from the Java class whom I hardly knew, he had their rate-of-success memorized as if he were a proud mother. I loved it.

Brandon had been asked to sit for a second interview with Plus Consulting. I do wonder, had he not had this in his pocket, if he would have been as fast and loose with the business of other people's interviews. Something tells me it wouldn't have mattered.

But in hindsight, it might have been better for the TE population to not know with such specificity who got what and when. From what I could gather, somewhere around six or seven students were contacted for second interviews. That meant that twenty-six people were not. Caitie was furiously busy with private student meetings, talking about ways they could follow up with these companies, ways to ensure that the next round of matchmaking went well, or just acting as a therapist, trying to calm down the pandemic of freak-out.

We came into the House of Metal on Friday to find the Elevate Space arranged with rows of chairs. There would be an impromptu meeting. We didn't hear from Kyle, the director of Tech Elevator, too often. Usually, when we needed to be addressed as a group, Caitie was the one to do the talking. But three days had passed since matchmaking and the place had descended into madness. Kyle took center stage.

Kyle was always clear and concise when he spoke, even though he used a lot of business-isms like "trust the process" and "you get out of it what you put into it." He and Caitie were far and away the most professional on the TE staff, though Kyle edged even Caitie by a bit. His speech was structured, well-thought-out, and to-the-point: everyone needs to chill the fuck out.

And he was right.

I realize that I was sitting pretty with a second interview, but even if I wasn't, panic time was a long way off. I didn't have a long history of job searching—but Jenny did and I bore witness to it. She would apply to places and not hear back for months sometimes, even when it ended positively with her getting an interview. And then even when she did get a callback, she might have another few months full of intense interviewing. She went through this mess several times over the course of the last decade, often ending up without a job offer. So, to start losing your mind because a company hadn't reached out after three days was completely unreasonable.

But, on the other hand, I understood the panic because I felt it too, even with my second interview secured. If this part of the experience didn't work out, then the whole, entire thing was a failure, a waste of time, a waste of money, and the possible ruination of a life. Dramatic? Yes. But in part, true.

Jason sat next to me while Kyle gave his speech, and throughout it his eyes were closed and he breathed deeply, his barrel chest rising and falling.

"You all right, bud?" I asked him after Kyle dismissed us.

Jason paused for a moment, his eyes closed. "No."

"What's up?" I asked. "Just nervous about the job hunt?"

"I'll be fine," he said.

I started to get the feeling that he might be having a panic attack. I had never really been around anyone who had panic attacks so I wasn't too keen on the signs. Jason was breathing heavily and wouldn't open his eyes.

"You'll be good, man. You're a really good coder."

"I know," he whispered between breaths.

"Do you need help or anything?"

"I'm fine."

So, I left him sitting there. Maybe I should have told someone, but I don't think Jason wanted me to. I went back and tried to work on the JavaScript homework, but I just ended up reading the email chain from Zoe again and then packing up my stuff. When I went out, Jason was still sitting there. His eyes were open now and he seemed calmer, scrolling through his phone while Kyle and Caitie cleaned up the Elevate Space, stacking the chairs around him.

| Chapter Eighteen |

THE most notable thing for me during the second matchmaking day was the lack of nauseous fear. There were still those in the cohort who were petrified, but that vibe in general was turned down a few notches. A week had passed since the first matchmaking day and a remarkable amount of students, more than twenty, had been asked to second interviews. FBK had interviewed fifteen students the previous week and had asked fourteen back for a second interview day. Yes, this made me feel less special and singled out, but I was still the only one who received a personal call from Zoe. That call grew more perplexing in my mind. There was basically no information that I got from it and everything I needed to know about the second interview I received from a mass email Zoe sent to all of the interviewees. My best guess was that I made a good impression on Meghan and she had told Zoe something vague, like, follow up with him. Not knowing what Meghan wanted exactly, Zoe just set up a call to "touch base," as they say, and repeated things that I already knew from the interview. Whatever the reason, I still counted it as a leg up on my fellow students.

The terrible thing about having fourteen of fifteen people get callbacks from FBK, it means that only one person was not asked back. And that poor soul was Christopher.

He was devastated. And rightly so, I think. What happened in the interview that had differentiated him from the others? How had fourteen been promising enough to speak with again and he had not? This was the question he wanted answered, particularly before going into the second round of matchmaking. After the emails had been sent from FBK, it took Christopher a day or two to figure out that he was the only one among the interviewees that was rejected. When this embarrassment was clear, Christopher and Caitie had a series of closed-door conversations about what might have happened. Christopher wanted Caitie to reach out to FBK for feedback so that if he had made some unforgivable faux pas he could be sure not to repeat it with other companies. Whatever came of these communications with FBK I don't know. But Christopher was not one of the students who was feeling calmer at matchmaking the second time around.

I personally felt flat the whole day for the second matchmaking. Last week, when I was in the grip of a holy terror, I was sharp and reactive. I felt utterly calm on this Tuesday and I think this calmness led me to be too casual in the interviews. You don't want to come off desperate, but you *really* don't want to seem like you don't want it. FBK had been my first choice and now that I had a second interview with them, there was a part of my subconscious that wanted to kick into a lower gear. I had one interview with a placement agency and another with Key Bank. The placement agency was friendly enough, but they're friendly with everyone. It's a numbers game with those people. They don't care if you can do the job, they just want to place you and collect their fee. The woman from Key Bank seemed utterly uninterested in our conversation and I, regrettably, did nothing to try and spark her interest.

"How did it go today?" I asked Christopher in the late afternoon.

"Better," he said nodding his head. "Better, I think."

He paused and then shrugged. "But I thought I did well last week too."

"You haven't heard anything back?"

"No," he said, looking directly into my eyes.

"Remember, ninety-two percent," I said.

This had become something of a rally call over the last two weeks. Tech Elevator had a 92 percent job placement. The chances of you converting the boot camp into a first job in tech were very, very good.

"Right, ninety-two percent," Christopher said with a wry smile. "Out of thirty-two students, that's two and a half who don't get jobs."

His math checked out.

"At this point, I'm pretty sure I'm one of those people."

"No. . ."

I thought he could be right. It wasn't fair, but he could be right. Christopher was the most educated person in the cohort. He graduated from the University of Michigan and then went to Russia as a Fullbright Scholar. After that, he achieved a master's degree from American University. He had been in final interviews with the United Nations before ultimately applying to Tech Elevator. This guy could definitely write automated tests for FBK. But something had gone wrong.

He was a Java student, so I had never worked with him, but from what I understood he was a pretty good programmer. But that's not what this stage of the experience was about. Counter-intuitively, being highly educated, clearly intelligent, and a good programmer were all secondary importances. These properties brought us success in the days leading up to matchmaking, but what got us to this point was not going to get us through the next leg. What we needed now were charisma, performance-under-pressure, and some good luck.

Christopher struggled mightily with his anxiety and I wondered how this was playing when he and his interviewers were behind closed doors. In a certain sense, he was very charismatic. He was funny and smart and insightful. But his personality and general aura were an acquired taste. Christopher was like jumping into a cool pool, shocking at first with its intensity, then enjoyable once you got used to it. But some people just won't stay in the pool long enough for it to feel good.

On Wednesday, everyone who had interviewed with FBK except for Christopher showed up to TE ready for their second interview. I remembered how I felt on the Reynolds interview day and figured that Christopher, if he had managed to get over his disappointment, was feeling raw about it all over again. I'm sorry to say I didn't try to float him any words of comfort. I was caught up in my own dramas and my own worries. I'm sure everyone else was too, and this probably made Christopher's day even more lonely.

The second interviews for FBK were not at the House of Metal. Instead, all fourteen students headed from the North Side to downtown, suited up and pin-prickly with nerves, to stand in the shadow cast by the FBK skyscraper, regularly called the Tech Tower. Some students drove, but driving into downtown Pittsburgh between the hours of nine and five o'clock is generally considered the work of lunatics. The rest of us took the T, a train system that serves as public transport for downtown Pittsburgh and a select few suburbs. It was a strange ride, everyone in their best clothes, some horsing around, others studying their notes, still others gazing pensively out at the moving skyline. Those around us who were not part of the group stared forward with earbuds inserted firmly, probably wondering what these hyper, overdressed goobs were doing and where they were going in the middle of the day.

The Tech Tower is massive. I had lived in New York City for some years, but those years were decidedly in the past. Outside Pittsburgh where I live, there are few buildings with more than three floors, so to be standing at the doorway of a thirty-three floor skyscraper was somewhat intimidating. Through the revolving doors, Zoe waited for us with two assistants. The tower was undergoing a renovation, so construction workers moved about as Zoe ushered us to the security sign-in, got us through the metal detectors and into the main lobby. There were two sets of six elevators, one set if you were going to floors one to eighteen and another if you were going higher.

"Where do we go, Zoe?" we asked.

"Thirty-three," she said. "All the way to the top."

All the way to the top, kid.

Of course we couldn't all fit in one elevator. We went in three batches, Zoe and her assistants splitting up to chaperone us to the crest of the world. I have issues with motion sickness and the ride on the T had not been good for me. Combined with my nerves and the elevator lift, I was feeling nice and queasy by the time I was shaking Meghan's hand just underneath the clouds.

The view out of the Tech Tower is impressive. We waited in a kitchenette gazing out the floor-to-ceiling windows down upon the Pittsburgh Pirates ballpark. There were cold cut sandwiches in the kitchenette, fruit, water, and coffee. Some people drank coffee and water, but no one ate a thing. I doubt anyone was hungry, but more importantly, the bad optics of sitting down and eating a sandwich with mustard moments before an interview, while the conductors of those interviews were drifting into the room, were more than any Caitie-Zajko-trained student would risk.

We were told that the festivities would begin in a few minutes and that we should stroll around the thirty-third floor and check out the digs. Craig and I walked together, like two meek supplicants who just showed up at the monastery. We were impressed. The floor-to-ceiling windows continued around the entire lap of the thirty-third floor, giving a 360-degree view of Pittsburgh from way, way up. There were the far-away cityscapes to admire, like the Pittsburgh Pirates Stadium or the road leading down to the Point where the three rivers converge, or the red incline cars slowly climbing the hills of Mt. Washington. But I liked to look at the city itself, peering straight down to Liberty Avenue or inspecting the Highmark Skyscraper only a few hundred yards away. I liked to imagine spotting Spider-Man perched in a crag of the US Steel Building, or the terrifying stomp of Godzilla smashing down 5th Avenue.

The offices themselves were sleek and cool, nicer than the glimpse we caught at the Microsoft building Craig and I had seen previously. There were no cubicles in the Tech Tower. It was open flooring, long blond desks with monitors and orange-cushioned chairs. There were meeting nooks in all the corners where one could close a door, but there were no solid walls. Everything was glass, everyone was visible all at once. It was the vision I had in my head of a tech office and, though I'm sure the Google and Facebook offices are cooler to the nth degree, this felt like the promised land.

When we made our circle back to the kitchenette, we were given a schedule. There was only one interview, but there were to be several informational talks with different groups from FBK, discussing the tools we would be using, a demonstration of automated testing, and HR related topics. As I looked over my schedule, a young man walked through the kitchenette area.

"Oh, this is Ralph," Meghan said. "He is a Tech Elevator graduate from Cleveland."

We stared at him, awestruck.

"Hi everyone," he waved. He was carrying a laptop and turned to go.

"Do you like your job?" someone called out from our group. I'm not sure who it was.

"Um, yeah," he said. "I do."

As if he could say anything else, standing in a room full of software managers. Ralph grimaced and then continued on to his desk.

This awkwardness cast a spell of silence over the crowd. All the TE students studied their schedules and those who would be interviewing us talked amongst themselves. Meghan stood alone, leaning against the counter. No one was talking to her, so I said hello.

I considered reintroducing myself because I knew she had met a lot of people in a short period of time, but I'm glad I didn't. She knew who I was.

We talked about personal things, mostly. The whole conversation lasted four or five minutes, but it came out that I had a wife and daughter and that Meghan had just gotten married. That was when I realized that I was almost definitely older than her, which was discombobulating. The power discrepancy during our sit-down interview had altered my vision, either adding years to Meghan or youth to myself. Now, I looked around the room and wondered how many of these people who would be deciding my fate were my juniors. It didn't really matter, but I wondered just the same.

My first hub during the round robin was concerned with software delivery tools. I knew my interview followed this demonstration, so it was difficult to pay attention. I tried to understand what a pipeline was and how it pertained to programming, but was largely unsuccessful. I was cognizant that though there was a dedicated time for my interview, I would still be judged during each hub of the interview day. So, though my brain was scrambled, I did my best to appear sharp and friendly and to remember people's names and use them when possible.

After the delivery tools, I found the office where I was to sit for my interview. I put my hand on the door, but, looking through, I could see that Kane was still speaking with the interview group. The interviewers noticed me at the door, so I smiled and backed away. Kane's interview overshot by five or six minutes and I knew that mine would most likely be shortened to get the schedule back on track. I counted this as a good thing.

There were four interviewers, which seemed excessive to me. I recognized one, Hank, who had spoken at Tech Elevator on DevOps day. Hank had been the first person I met from FBK. His talk that day had started the ball rolling toward the eventuality of FBK becoming my number one choice. We talked after the panel at TE and exchanged emails as well. I felt close to him, but when we shook hands I could tell he barely remembered me.

This was considered a technical interview, which scared the hell out of me. I didn't see a computer in the room, nor a whiteboard, so I was pretty sure I wasn't going to be given a coding problem. And then, when the questions started coming, I realized that I had heard most of them. This comforted me at the time, but later during some introspection, I began to wonder. I don't know which way the information flowed, but it seemed to me that either FBK was asking the interview questions that Tech Elevator supplied them or that Tech Elevator somehow knew exactly what FBK was going to ask us and had been feeding us the information for months. Either way, I had the answers to most of the questions down rote and was able to answer them as easily as any trained parrot. The interview was a breeze.

I am one of those lucky people who, in a social situation with pressure, can often find a place of calmness. This doesn't translate to the physical side of things, mind you. I'm adequately athletic, but in the midst of anything competitive I tend to freeze up. I was a pretty bad high school athlete even though my skills at the sports I played were decent. It's just the opposite when I am put on the spot socially. If it comes down to it, I can be trusted to say the right thing at the right time. Not always. But usually.

Either way, I walked out of the interview feeling ten feet tall.

Next I was back with a group of students for the talk on benefits and general human resources. I entered the room and was pleased to see Zoe. It's strange how close I felt to these characters whom I viewed as helping me along my way. Taking a step back, Zoe had done nothing more than be pleasant during an interview. But I felt as if she was a true, deep friend who was, right now, coming through for me when I was in a tight spot. And maybe it was due to this unbalanced perspective that I was taking toward FBK and the interview process, but she seemed to greet me warmer than the others. Maybe she and Meghan really did like me more than everybody else. It's possible.

I was very happy with the HR discussion. Zoe covered all the general amenities—health care, 401k opportunities, and the like. But I had expected all those things. What made me sit up and say,

"Ooh" was the three weeks of vacation we would start with. Yes, I realize the irony in wanting a new job and being mainly excited about the time I could spend not being there. But I really like having vacation days.

At Barnes & Noble, I had racked up four weeks of vacation over the sixteen years that I worked there. And that amount was what I felt I needed. I want to get to October or November and find myself saying "What am I going to spend this last week on?" After I was laid off and made the move to Green Basil, I started with no vacation. After six months I got one fucking week. Green Basil had been completely accommodating when I was sick and in the hospital with diverticulitis, but I still would have had just one week's vacation the following year. And I was in a management position. That infuriated me.

Three weeks to begin at FBK. And, really, it's more than that. Like many reasonable companies, they have "occasional absence" days instead of "sick" days. At Barnes & Noble, if I wanted to use a sick day I had to either actually be sick or pretend to be sick and call out at the last minute, screwing up the store's plans for the day. It's a terrible system. I often ended the year not using all of my sick days and being disgruntled about it. With occasional absence days, I don't have to participate in the childish act of feigning illness. I just schedule the day off. I can even do it in advance. With six of these paid time off days to begin with and two personal days, the three weeks was actually four weeks and three days. The paid time off that it took me sixteen years to accumulate at Barnes & Noble, I would have my first day at FBK.

"Man, I'm hungry," Craig said as we exited the rotating doors into the kicked ant hill that was Liberty Avenue at one o'clock in the afternoon. "Do you want to grab something to eat before we hop on the train?"

Drew overheard us. "We're going to Moe's!"

He was jogging to catch up with Jack, Brandon, and Fancy about half a block ahead of us. Drew and Jack loved Taco Bell. Since there wasn't one close by, it looked like Moe's was going to be a stand in.

"What do you think?" I asked Craig.

He shrugged his shoulders. "Sure."

We strolled along slowly, talking about our interview experiences and seeing downtown Pittsburgh in the daylight. Normally, the only reason I would come downtown was for a baseball game or to go to a restaurant, both night-time activities. Craig thought his interview was awkward but went well as far as the technical parts were concerned. Like me, he thought the questions were pretty easy, especially coming off of the Reynolds interview. But, as we had each heard in the last half hour, not all of the TE students had the same experience.

There were several different groups of FBK representatives conducting interviews. Not all of these groups got the memo about asking easy interview questions that we had previously memorized. After some serious sleuthing, it was determined that those who had had their interviews in office 4-A had gotten pummeled with questions they had no shot of answering. There was one particular question about a "try/catch" strategy that no one could figure out the right answer to, even after we put our heads together wondering what the interviewers had wanted to hear. I felt fortunate to have avoided this much more difficult line of questioning, and weakly fatalistic in that my success or ruin may have come down to the luck of the draw.

"Whoa," Craig said, stopping in his tracks.

I stopped with him and followed his eyes to the sign three feet above us that read "Sushi One." The entire storefront of the restaurant was about the length of a picnic table with nothing inside but a service counter, three round tables, and another counter wrapping around the walls to stand and eat.

"Oh, yeah," I said.

The Moe's group was a full block ahead of us.

"They'll figure it out," Craig said.

We turned in to Sushi One and ordered rolls and seaweed. We stood at our table in the center of the tiny restaurant in our nice suits, eating with chopsticks, watching crowds of people go by in the middle of a work day.

"I think I would come here a lot if I worked at FBK," I told Craig.

"Me too, man," Craig said, looking around, almost giddy. "For sure."

| Chapter Nineteen |

THERE was still another capstone, believe it or not. Just when you thought you could turn your attention fully to the job hunt, the most difficult task of the entire cohort reared its ugly head, like the big boss at the end of a video game, demanding your time and concentration. The penultimate capstone was meant to test all of our skills. Capstone Four was a reckoning.

So I decided to game the system.

One lesson I learned from the previous capstones was that you were made and unmade by whom you were paired with. I had been pretty fortunate through the first three: Arjun, Jack, and Brandon. Arjun and Brandon were close enough to me in skill that it didn't feel like anyone had to be carried across the finish line. Jack, on the other hand, had been waiting at the finish line as I came panting toward it, wondering what took me so long. I don't think I held Jack back or annoyed him during Capstone Two, but maybe I did and he was just cool about it. Either way, up until now I had nothing to complain about for capstone partners. I wanted to keep it that way.

I had witnessed several solid programmers matched with people who were struggling. In these situations, the ones who were stronger basically did the capstone by themselves. Or, in some cases, got overwhelmed and turned in terrible work. I was definitely worried about getting stuck on a rough team. I didn't want anything to distract me from the job hunt.

Some weeks before, Bill had offhandedly said this tidbit about the final capstone:

"So, you can make up your own project, if you like. It has to be approved by me and I might add some requirements. And you might not like the requirements. But you can do it. In the past, we've had students form their own teams and make their own projects."

Form their own teams, you say?

I took note of this.

The task of the final capstone was to build a full app. It was to have a database that we would fill, a front end of our own design, and a back end connecting the two and adding functionality. There was a menu from which you could choose fleshed out ideas that Tech Elevator provided—things like a brewery-finder, an educational flashcard app, recipe-making apps. The way the teams were to be formed was similar to the way the matchmaking event had been scheduled. You were to write down the top three applications that you were interested in building and then those who voted similarly were put on a team of four with you.

My wife works in digital marketing for a franchise. Her boss and owner of the company at the time was exploring the possibility of building a website that could match people who are interested in buying a franchise with the franchise that most suits their needs. The site would have insider information on these franchises and those interested would subscribe for a fee and then pay a finding cost if they were matched with a franchise. This sounded pretty similar to the apps on the menu for Capstone Four. There would be a front end to click through and search your franchises by different criteria, a database with the info on the franchises, and a form to sign up for the service. And as a cool bonus, if we made a good enough app, maybe Jenny's boss would use it. And as a double cool bonus, if I pitched this idea, I could form my own team.

It didn't exactly work out like that. What Bill described as being "able to build your own team" wasn't completely accurate. The way it shook out was that my Franchise Finder app was added to the menu of apps that people could vote on. I told Bill I was forming a team and in return he told me to make sure all four members put the Franchise Finder as their number one and everything should work out. But I started to get worried when a handful of people told me that they were putting Franchise Finder as their number one choice, several whom I wasn't completely keen on working with.

After the voting was in, I peeked my head into Bill's office. It was the end of the day on a Friday and he was getting some overdue grading done.

"Got a minute?"

"Yeah, what's up, Sean?"

I explained to him that I had formed the idea for Franchise Finder with three specific students and now it looked like there was a possibility that they could get locked out of their own idea due to the voting. It wasn't 100 percent true; the Franchise Finder was my idea, or, more accurately, Jenny's boss's idea, but still. I had an agreement with a super team, which I had done some work to unite.

Bill said he'd see what he could do.

For whatever reason, this caused me a lot of stress. I think I was nearing the end of my stores of strength and fortitude for the boot camp. I felt drained. The second interview with FBK was over a week old now and I hadn't heard anything back except for bland email responses to my thank-you notes. It was somewhat absurd to expect a response within a week, but I had been expecting an email or phone call any moment since I exited the revolving doors of the Tech Tower. None of the other companies that I had interviewed with had contacted me about a second interview. I still had some JavaScript homework hanging around that I did not understand and would have to complete over the weekend. And if this capstone didn't pan out the way I was angling it to, I could be in for two weeks of immense struggle.

I was so clouded with thought on the way home that I didn't even realize it was the last day of class.

Twelve weeks. Sixty lessons. And now all that was left was two week's time and the final capstone.

Last day of class. A reason to celebrate, right? But what, exactly, am I celebrating? None of it mattered if FBK, or somebody, *anybody*, didn't contact me and offer me a job or more interviews. Those sixty days of toil were a waste if a company did not hire me. Not only did I have fifteen thousand dollars on the line, but my ego was being offered up too. If I quit a full-time job and paid all this money to enroll in a program and then got nothing for it, then the narrative for now and forever would be that I got scammed. Or that I was too stupid to make the program work for me, even though 92 percent of the people did. Or both of these things. If I didn't get a job out of this, I would end up wallowing in self-pity, maybe for years as I slowly tried to pay off the bills. Everyone close to me would think that I had acted thoughtlessly, that I wasn't a functioning adult, that I had squandered every ounce of assistance given me. I had put myself in a position where powers beyond my control could leave me stranded in a realm of depression and debt and embarrassment.

But at least I got my super team.

When I came into the House of Metal on Monday, I checked our chat channel and found the Franchise Finder listing: Me, Matt, Fancy, and of course, my boy Craig. Super crew!

The whole team had interviewed at FBK, but both Fancy and Matt were in deep with Single Source second interviews. Also, it appeared as if Reynolds was interested in Craig. This would break up our work a bit, as obligations for interviews and coding tests pulled rank on the Franchise Finder. But I was sure that we were going to have the easiest time of any capstone group.

The final capstone had some other trappings beyond just building the app. We were doing a mock work project. It was a simulation of what we would do at an actual job. So, for this, we were assigned !Bill as our scrum master and Caitie as our Product Owner.

The position of scrum master has nothing to do with rugby. The scrum master is someone who organizes a development team and leads the meetings. The scrum master works closely with the developers and acts as a conduit between them and management.

The Product Owner, or PO as the acronym-obsessed business world likes to say, is just what it sounds like. They have complete ownership of the product being made. They must have a thorough understanding of the business details and communicate those details, with the help of the scrum master, to the developers. They will often have a demo once or twice a week to see what the developers are working on and give critiques, guiding them along the path to completion.

We had a good architectural plan going into our first standup meeting with !Bill, but I don't think that the meeting went the way she wanted. She was trying to introduce us to ticket-based working and the Agile work methodology, but we just weren't following. Agile is probably too much to get into here, but just know that it's a way of working intended to facilitate two things: it makes communication pertaining to who is doing what very clear, and it makes it easy to switch from one task to another quickly without leaving a mess of unfinished work behind.

Ticket-based development is pretty simple. Large problems are broken down into many small tasks, each task is represented in a "story." During a planning session, developers will "take stories" for the week and these will be the tasks they have to accomplish. The scrum master or the developer will work a board, moving their tickets from "not done" to "in progress" to "done," writing comments all the way describing any problems or "blockers" they've run into that are slowing them down. It's a great way to work. And the super team did not get it.

"We have a plan," Matt told !Bill.

"OK," she said. "So we should take the plan and break it down into stories."

"All right," Matt said, looking at his sheet. "Craig is good at database stuff, so he's going to do that. Rick is going to work on the logic for the front end, and me and Sean will do the back end. Sean's going to do the CSS work too. So, four stories."

"Um. No," !Bill said. "Those tickets are way too big. They're actually four epics."

"Epics? All right, then. Four epics."

Matt closed his notebook. We pushed our chairs out and made to leave the meeting room.

!Bill put her head in her hands. "Sit down."

We sat back down.

"So, for the database, what is the first thing Craig needs to do?" !Bill prodded.

Matt looked around the table at us, a bewildered expression on his face. He was answered by raised eyebrows and shrugged shoulders. We shared his bewilderment.

Matt tried to answer !Bill. "I don't know, make the database? I'm not getting it."

It went on like this for some time. Eventually !Bill got us to break down the big chunks of work that Matt had described into smaller tasks, but we didn't really use the board that she provided. We just talked it out, all four of us working hard but not really together at the beginning. !Bill was never able to completely wrangle us into correctly performing ticket-based development, but she backed off when she saw our progress during demos.

During the demos, our super crew was being pretty super. We started on Monday and by Friday we had a fully fleshed out database hooked up to the front end. You could already search the franchises in the search bar. And we still had five days with nothing to do but tinker with it. No other team was even close to this far along.

While other teams were working through the weekend, the four of us relaxed, came in Monday and worked a half day because Craig had a final interview at Reynolds and both Fancy and Matt were in final interviews for Single Source.

On Tuesday, I arrived at the House of Metal at quarter after eight. No one else from the team was there yet, so I set up my computer where we had been sitting together and planned to tinker with the colors and fonts of the website for a little bit. When my computer was up and running I first checked my email. There was a message from Zoe.

Good morning Sean!

I hope this email finds you well. If you have the opportunity, please give me a phone call today. I just wanted to reconnect with you regarding the opportunities within our DevOps team!

I will mostly be available this afternoon if you can chat then.

Notice how the email gently hints that I shouldn't call her until the afternoon? I called at 8:30 a.m.

She answered even though she wasn't at work yet. Zoe was walking from the bus to the Tech Tower, the cacophony of downtown Pittsburgh rumbling behind her.

"Hello?"

"Hi, Zoe! It's Sean Rogers."

"Oh, hi, Sean. Good morning."

"Yeah, good morning. I was just calling about your email?"

"Sure! I can't talk right now, I'm on my way to work. Could we set up a time? Maybe four o'clock?"

God damn it. Four o'clock? That's like a million hours from now.

"Four o'clock will be great. Do you want me to call you?"

"I'll call you."

"That's a job offer," Matt said when I told him about the call.

"Right?" I said

"Definitely."

Jenny thought so too.

"Remember, you can't say 'yes' right away. Get the salary number and the details and we'll talk about it."

And Caitie basically confirmed it.

"It certainly sounds like she's going to make you an offer."

She was smiling so hard that I thought her teeth might crack.

"I've wanted to tell you for weeks."

"You knew?"

"Not a hundred percent. But, yes. You were always first on the list of people FBK wanted to offer."

So that was it. I had to sit on my hands until 4:00 p.m. and then someone was going to offer me a large amount of money to write code. If you rewound my life six months, you would see me carrying crates of apples off of a truck behind a grocery store.

It was a long day. We had some buttoning up to do on the Franchise Finder and I did not contribute at all. No one was mad at me. They understood.

Caitie scheduled me a room to take Zoe's call. At 3:45 p.m. I sat in the empty office by myself with a notepad, a pen, and a cup of coffee, which I was planning to let grow cold. I sat there in total silence for fifteen minutes. When four o'clock came, I stared at my phone, scared to touch it because I might accidentally reject Zoe's call and scared to not touch it because I should probably check that there isn't something wrong with it. At 4:01 p.m. I started calling Zoe swear words in my mind. The phone vibrated at 4:02 p.m.

We exchanged some pleasantries, but Zoe got to the point pretty quick.

"So, we would like to extend you an offer to work at FBK."

A sense of surreality hit. My mind felt strangely similar to when I had been laid off from Barnes & Noble, a flushed face and buzzing numbness at the top of my head. Really good news and really bad news hit me the same way.

"That's great," I managed to reply.

"And the salary we're offering is sixty thousand dollars a year," she continued.

I laughed out loud. This was $24,000 more a year than I had been making four months prior. If a $60,000 salary doesn't impress you, I'm sure a more than 65 percent increase in a salary does. It was life-altering. I couldn't imagine $60,000. I thought of the nights Brandon stayed at my house, up late, fantasizing about money. In my mind's eye, I saw us walking into the Dollar Store, throwing our cash around like some real big shots.

Zoe went on to talk about health care and paid time off and 401ks, but I was in dreamland. I figured she would send it all in an email to me eventually.

"So, how does that sound?" Zoe asked.

I realized I was supposed to say something.

"It sounds fantastic," I said.

"OK, well, we can send you an official offer. . ."

"Oh! I'm not supposed to accept right now," I said.

“I’m sorry?” Zoe asked.

“I told my wife I would wait a day and talk it over with her before I accepted anything.”

“Of course!” Zoe said. “I will send you the details of the offer in an email and you two can look it over. Take your time. Call me back when you’re ready.”

“I mean, I’ll be calling you tomorrow,” I admitted. “I just promised I wouldn’t accept on the spot.”

Job-hunting tip for you: It’s always best to negotiate from a place of strength.

“OK. . . ” Zoe said.

“Thanks, Zoe.”

“Thank *you*, Sean.”

I basically peaced out on the capstone. I couldn’t concentrate. I hung with Craig for a while, who seemed almost happier than me that I got the offer, and then I went home early. Jenny wasn’t back from work yet and Afton was still at school. I walked around the house. Should I celebrate? Drink a beer or something? I couldn’t settle on anything. Eventually I sat down with a calculator and figured out how much more $60,000 was than my salary at Green Basil by the month, the week, the day. I got deep into the minutia of how many bills we had and how much extra there would be after we paid them. Made a couple of different saving strategies. That was a good time.

The best way to celebrate, it turned out, was by telling other people. Jenny already knew of course, but Afton was pretty excited about it. I wasn’t sure if she would grasp the difference this made for our lives. Hell, I’m not sure I grasped the difference this would make for our lives. But she seemed to understand that something big had happened. She told me she was proud of me. Then she went and played barbies on the porch, talking to herself like a lunatic for nearly an hour.

Besides the relief and joy that Jenny felt, telling my parents was the next best thing. They had loaned me $3,000 to help with the expenses of the school. If I were them, I would have been very concerned about the legitimacy of the program. But I heard nothing even close to doubt from them the whole time. Every word from their mouths during those four months were words of support and the only time they mentioned the money was to say that I should take my time paying it back. My parents are financially comfortable, but they're not people who can throw around three grand like it's chump change. Money can sometimes be a symbol and this money symbolized their confidence in me.

I told them in person, but I don't exactly remember what they said. It was a good moment. But, better than that, every few months and probably for the rest of my life, my dad will say to me regarding Tech Elevator, "Boy, that sure was a good decision." This is a guy who has witnessed a lot of my bad decisions, so it is immensely satisfying to know that when he saw me with my back against the wall, I made the right move. I paid my parents back that $3,000 before the summer was out.

There was a lot of talk about negotiating leading up to and after the matchmaking. We had been told by the teachers that if you push back on a salary, a lot of these companies will cave. And if they don't, no one's mad. This is business. They'll still hire you for their original offer. At one point while discussing this with Jenny, we had come to the conclusion that I should push back on *any* salary, just to see what happened. And maybe I should have. But I didn't.

Firstly, the money was more than enough. Caitie told me coming in that the average salary for the graduating students was over

$58,000 thousand and that that number was actually higher in the Pittsburgh market. I don't know if I didn't fully believe her or if I thought that for some reason I wouldn't be able to wrangle that type of job, but I truly expected low $50,000s. I didn't want to push back on $60,000. It felt disrespectful to the company and somehow, it felt disrespectful to my own accomplishment. Like I had been searching for a chest of treasure and when I finally found it, I raised my eyebrows and said, "That's it?"

I accepted the job the next day, first on the phone with Zoe and then officially over email because she asked me to. Yes, there was a drug test and yes, I passed. I think the last time I smoked was August of the prior year, putting a full eight months between those puffs and the screening. During the wait period between the peeing and the results, I called my friend Adeep who had Houdini'd his way through many drug tests as he climbed the ranks in his financial company. When I described my predicament, he laughed.

"Eight months? You're *totally* cool," he assured me. "Wow, we're both bankers now!"

I still freaked out until it came back clean. But it did. Of course it did.

So, I was the first one. Not the first to get an offer, that distinction belonged to Drew. But I was the first Tech Elevator student of my cohort to accept a job offer. Jenny and I said that this accomplishment should be given the Zajko Award. Some weeks later we told Caitie this over drinks in a bar and she turned bright red laughing. I don't know whether she liked the idea or not.

On Wednesday, both Matt and Fancy were offered jobs from Single Source. Then, on Thursday, in the morning, Matt was offered a job at FBK, too, as was Craig. I was through the roof. Not only did I land my first-pick-job, but now Matt and Craig were going to be with me? I envisioned Craig and I eating at Sushi One so much that we wouldn't like sushi anymore.

Then, some hours later, Craig got an offer from Reynolds. Like, a big, big offer. Yes, I do know what the offer was, but I won't say because Craig is more private than me about his money. But, a simple deduction will tell you that it blew away the $60,000 that FBK was serving up.

"I mean, I like, *have* to take this, right?" Craig said to our capstone group.

"You don't have to," I said.

Yes, I was definitely motivated by the personal desire to work with Craig. But I meant what I said.

"Do you want to drive all the way out there every day?"

Remember, the Reynolds headquarters was approximately thirty-five minutes outside of Pittsburgh.

"I don't think I'd mind," Craig said.

"I would take it," Matt said. "That money is a different level of lifestyle."

"And it sounds like it's straight development," Fancy put in. "The FBK stuff would be automated testing."

Fancy was right. More than most students in the cohort, Craig was purely in this coding boot camp for the code. He had already been making pretty good money in his former career. He had quit and attended Tech Elevator because he wanted, more than anything else, to write software. Automated testing was definitely a form of programming, but it was baby steps that led up to harder things. I needed those baby steps, Craig did not. He was ready to run.

By Friday, the super team was employed. The first four students to accept jobs were all sitting at the same table, working on the same project. Well, not working. We'd already finished. Maybe one of my skills is that I'm good at recognizing talent? I don't know. Could I monetize that?

Fancy went to Single Source, Matt signed with me to FBK, and Craig accepted at Reynolds Sportswear. We came into TE on Friday even though the Franchise Finder was completely finished. By ten o'clock in the morning we had put our computers away, cracked really expensive beers that Fancy had bought for us, and played Settlers of Catan.

Things went off the rails later that day. Someone (pretty sure it was Drew) changed the rusted, antiquey letters in the window that said "ELEVATE" to "EAT VEEL." Offers were coming in all over the place. You could tell who was doing well by whether or not they had a beer in their hand. A young kid named Charlie was a couple deep when he was called to an interview in downtown Pittsburgh at some company who made tech for car dealerships. He was half in the bag and had pizza sauce on his white shirt when he left. He came back with a job paying $55,000.

After Fancy destroyed us at Catan, we hit the rooftop to drink more beer. Someone made a run to Beirs Tavern and spent a small fortune on growlers. I drank porters until I was sunburned and then stood around talking to Craig while we waited to sober up so we could drive home.

"So," Craig said. "It's pretty crazy that this actually worked."

"Yeah," I agreed. "I guess I thought it would, that's why I signed up. But still..."

It's not often that life presents a clear milestone where one can stop, look around, and say "I did it." But this was definitely a moment like that. I had taken a huge risk, worked inhumanly hard for four months, developed a skill from scratch, and turned that skill into a high-paying career. Yes, there was some anxiety about starting the job at FBK. There was some anxiety about how these skills would translate and if I would actually be able to perform in a professional setting. But I didn't start at FBK for two weeks. I didn't have to worry about that just yet. For now, I felt pretty good about my spot in the world. I felt accomplished. I felt smart.

An Epilogue in Three Parts

Part One: Privilege

I'm white, did I mention that? No, I didn't. But I didn't have to. You knew.

In this book I covered one difficult year. I got laid off, I was briefly stuck in a job I didn't like, I got sick, and then I took a financial risk to receive more education in a way that was intense and challenging. And through these trying times, the color of my skin was a benefit to me. The ease with which I've always found work can in part be attributed to my good attitude and the way that I present myself. But part of that presentation is being a white male. I remember one of my high school jobs, walking into a toy store and being hired before I filled out the application. I barely said anything. The manager looked at me and asked if I could start the next day. In the predominately white Pittsburgh neighborhood, would this have happened if I had black or brown skin? I don't think so.

I didn't have to interview for Green Basil either, not really. And that was a management position. The Green Basil store director, whom I had worked with at Barnes & Noble pulled me aside before the interview and told me the job was mine if I wanted it. And while I was appreciative, I almost didn't take the job, because three months after laying me off, Barnes & Noble was still paying me severance. How likely would I have been to land in this position of strength had I been a minority in America? Not likely, I think.

And I should also address the money with which I paid to attend Tech Elevator. Like I said earlier, my parents loaned me $3,000. But the real difference-maker in the decision of whether to attend Tech Elevator or not was that when Jenny's father passed away, we received an inheritance, enough to cover the cost of the school with some left over. That money, when inspected, also came from a place of privilege. Jenny's father was a very hard-working man who dedicated his life to building his real estate business. He was also a man who liked to tell stories, and at least one of those stories illustrate that during the '70s and '80s he was able to get deals and loans from a small bank in Ohio because he knew the people who worked at the bank. These were generous, good-ol-boy loans that happened in small-town rural America. Money changed hands without much due diligence. And the money that changed hands would have stayed in the bank had the hands been black.

Russ made many smart decisions and worked like crazy for that money and Jenny and I appreciate every penny. But whiteness played a role in his success and Jenny's inheritance is a privilege not often afforded other races in America. The inheritance comes from a place of white privilege and this is the money that we invested in Tech Elevator, which now affords us a middle-class lifestyle.

It's very easy to attribute my own successes purely to personal skills and decisions. It makes me feel good to think that I am clever enough and talented enough to get what I want. And these attributes actually are, in fact, part of the key to my success. I haven't been exactly humble when discussing my natural talents and my work ethic in the previous pages. But those good attributes are made visible by my white skin to employers whereas the same attributes are often muted with minority applicants because of the long-standing and deep-seated nature of American bigotry and the general crowning of straight, white men.

While America is over 13 percent black, only 6 percent work in the tech industry. While women make up more than 50 percent of the United States population, they make up less than 12 percent of software developers.

Jenny and I, like much of America, have been spurred into introspection by the Black Lives Matter protests of 2020 and, also, by the blatant racist rhetoric coming from the White House. Actions are louder than words, so Jenny and I, in the summer of 2020 founded the Tech Elevator Alumni Scholarship[3], which gives money to womxn and minorities attending TE to cover a portion of the tuition. I've wanted to volunteer for a long time but never settled on anything. I know Tech Elevator works and can change lives. I thought this was as good a place as any to begin being charitable. We will give away our first thousand dollars in September of 2020 and are working with other former students to make that amount higher for the next cohort.

[3]If you are a Tech Elevator graduate and would like to contribute, go to https://tealumni.com/

Part Two: Covid-19

Well, this sure stinks, doesn't it?

It is July 21, 2020, and as I write this the United States is adding more than sixty thousand cases a day to the tally of those who have been infected with the coronavirus. So far, the virus has not hurt or killed anyone directly in my life, but I am aware that that day could come. Allegheny County, the Pennsylvanian county that contains Pittsburgh, has so far been fortunate as compared to many other U.S. cities.

We had a vacation scheduled in March of 2020; we took Afton to Puerto Rico. When we left, it was clear that the coronavirus was going to be a serious thing, when we returned the world had closed. Both Jenny and I are very fortunate in that we haven't lost our jobs. We've been working from home since we returned from that vacation. I was able to grow a really nice, long beard, which was one of the bright spots. But it got itchy, so I shaved.

I did not like working from home at the beginning of the quarantine. I had been working from home on Fridays for nearly a year, but every day of the week was too much for me. I was still learning and needed to see people face-to-face, be in the same room, to figure out some of my more technical problems.

At least, that's how I felt then. I don't feel that way now. I don't know exactly what changed. Maybe I got a little better at the job, maybe the job got a little easier, maybe I just calmed down and needed some time for the peaceful effect of acceptance to sink it. At this point, I don't care if I ever go back. I can sleep in till 6:00 a.m. and still get my writing done. And if I eat lunch while working, I can use my lunch break to go for a run. You know I like that.

I would label working from home a little slice of heaven were it not for how the quarantine is affecting Afton. The cyber-schooling in the Spring of 2020 was not good. The school was caught off guard, just like everyone else, and couldn't get it together to provide real education for the remainder of the year. There was a website where some assignments were listed. Afton blew through them in an hour or so each day. Her teacher had a video chat with the kids for half an hour every Wednesday and that was it for contact. It was financially a blessing for Jenny and me to both be working during a crisis like this, but for Afton's sake it might have been better if one of us were laid off. We struggle to engage with her during the day and she wanders around the house like a wraith while we type on our computers, hangs in the doorways while we talk on meetings.

It was worse at the beginning because we were quarantined even from my parents who usually take her during the weekdays in the summer. One afternoon in April she came downstairs, sat at the dining room table where I work, and cried because she was so bored. Literally bored to tears. I started taking off a day every other week so that I could spend it with her, but it wasn't enough. And I couldn't do that forever.

It's a little better now, as we've added my parents back into our lives and a few select friends for Afton. But she is still bored most of the time and she watches a ridiculous amount of television, something we were pretty strict about in the before-times. I worry about her mental health more than anything else these days.

But, as with every other part of life, we deal with what is served to us. Things are not as bad as they could be and our fate is still in our own hands if we choose to guide it. Hopefully, someday soon, this pandemic will be in the past. Instead of being our current reality it will just be one hell of a story.

Part Three: Job Round-Up

Let's start with me, since I am the subject of this book. I was hired by FBK at the end of April 2019 to write automated tests with the DevOps team. There are many different aspects of my job, but the main task is to write code that automatically clicks through a website validating certain functionalities or to write tests that make calls to APIs, validating that the response we get back is what we expected. There is a lot of documentation involved and I had some months of struggle around January and February of 2020. But things have evened out now. In fact, I would say they are going much, much better than expected. I received a bonus in December, which shocked me. I was given a raise in the spring, which was expected but still nice. And then this summer I was promoted from one who writes automated tests to one who manages a small group of automated testers. That was the biggest surprise of all.

I'm just starting this new position. In fact, I have meetings all day today with the teams I'll be in charge of. It's a bit stressful, but I've learned to do what I can, educate myself as much as possible, and above all remain calm in the face of the wave.

But enough about me.

FBK ended up making many offers and many of my school buddies now work with me. Rob, who I sat next to the first day and who looks like Jon Snow, works with me at FBK. As does Jack, the nineteen-year-old wiz kid whom I worked with on Capstone Two. Arjun, my Capstone One partner, got a job at HealthNet and then eventually moved over to FBK at the beginning of 2020. Kane, the boxer, now lives the dream at FBK. I already said that Matt accepted a job at FBK, and, all-in-all, twelve students from Cohort[2] collect paychecks from the Tech Tower.

Drew, after many interviews and offers, accepted a job at CGI. Also with more offers than fingers on one hand was Brandon. Brandon seemed to get a lucrative job offer after every interview. He ended up accepting at GNC. Diane was offered FBK, but decided to work at a small firm called Plus Consulting. Mr. Rick Fancy works at Single Source. Wayne, the student who had the hardest time learning the code, now works at Highmark. Jason, the chef who sat behind Craig and me, struggled for a bit to find employment, but eventually got in as a software developer at 84 Lumber.

Of the thirty-two students in Cohort [2] of Tech Elevator Pittsburgh, thirty were hired within a couple months of graduating, many within a few weeks, and many before the actual graduation. This success can be attributed to our hard work and to the skill and tenacity of our teachers; but in my estimation, the heaviest lifting was done by Caite Zajko. It is an amazing thing, I think, to take thirty people who know nothing, or very little, about technology and land them well-paying, entry-level technology jobs within five months of meeting them. She performs this trick three times a year. She is nothing short of astonishing.

Two students did not find jobs within six months. One declined to be interviewed for the book, but as I understand it, he just started working in a tech position this summer, a little more than a year after leaving Tech Elevator. The other, unfortunately, was Christopher.

Christopher is now gainfully employed and making good money, but it was a slog. Possibly the highest level of pure intelligence and certainly the most educated, he didn't get hired until November of 2019, seven months after graduating. And this was a painful seven months. Caitie continued to work with him, but their relationship frayed as Christopher grew more and more despondent and embarrassed with his lot.

But these dark times are in the past. He now works for a fin-tech company in Pittsburgh. He was upbeat when I spoke with him in early July of 2020, psyched that he could work at home full-time, and looking to buy property in Washington state where he plans to build a house next to a lake. So, all's well that ends well.

I still come in contact with many of the TE people who work at FBK. The bank continued to hire aggressively during subsequent cohorts, so now you can't throw a keyboard without hitting a recent graduate of the boot camp. It's nice. I love throwing keyboards. And I love working with other boot campers. I know their struggle and they know mine.

Outside of work, I still keep in touch with Craig, Brandon, and Matt. GNC headquarters is just around the block from the Tech Tower and Brandon and I used to grab lunch or an after-work drink a few times a month until the stupid fucking cornona virus came and ruined everything. I haven't seen him since the quarantine.

I work with Matt, but I also play tennis with him occasionally. We try to play every other weekend, but it's more like every three or four months. People get busy, y'know?

And Craig? Craig's my dude. I see him every couple of weeks. Sometimes we grab sushi dinners together, other times we hang out at Craig's house to strum our guitars and play Magic the Gathering. Yes, I play Magic now. The nerds wore me down. You should play it, too, though. It's really fun.

Acknowledgments

A special thanks to Chastity West, who helped me in three ways: by being an early reader, by introducing me to my eventual publisher, and by editing the manuscript. Clearly, this book wouldn't exist if not for you. Thank you to Allison Randal and Onyx Neon.

Thanks to the Tech Elevator staff for all that you did for me and for what you continue to do for the students in your program. Special thanks to Caitie Zajko for your earnest excitement and for sitting for multiple interviews. Thank you to all others who were interviewed for this book.

Thanks to my early readers, to Josh Pringle who taught me how to use "which" and "that" properly, to Luke Brooks, who fixed up my code in this book (and also carried me through my first year of work), and to Tim Pitoniak, who has read everything I've written since I was eighteen. Thanks to Billy Mott, Laura Miller, Michael Naccarelli, and Elizabeth Velardo.

Finally, thank you to Tim and Marilyn Rogers and to Russ and Cindy Gabel. Your support makes mine, Jenny, and Afton's life possible.

END

CPSIA information can be obtained
at www.ICGtesting.com
Printed in the USA
LVHW032059310721
693989LV00004B/118

9 780985 451981